Moonlight Rose in Blue:
Collected Poems

1971-2024

David Cope

Grand River Poetry Press
Grand Rapids, Michigan

Copyright and Publication

Copyright © 1971-2024 by David Cope.
Cover Photo by Rob Beahan.

Library of Congress Cataloging-in-Publication Data:

Cope, David 1948-
    Moonlight Rose in Blue: Collected Poems by David Cope
    453 pages.

"After Ronsard" (p. 225) is adapted from Pierre de Ronsard's Sonnet 26 from the second book of *Sonnets Pour Helene.*

"After Lope" (p. 245) is adapted from Poem I of *Rimas Humanos.*

ISBN: 978-1-968226-00-8

Published by Grand River Poetry Press. Grand Rapids, MI
grandriverpoetrycollective.com

For Suzanne

Dearest Companion

Works by David Cope

Books

Quiet Lives. Foreword by Allen Ginsberg (1983)
On The Bridge (1986)
Fragments from the Stars (1990)
Coming Home (1993)
Silences for Love (1998)
Turn the Wheel (2003)
Masks of Six Decades (chapbook, 2010)
The Train: Howl *in Chicago* (chapbook, 2017)
The Invisible Keys: New and Selected Poems (2017)
A Bridge Across the Pacific: Leaves for Chen Zi'ang, Guan Yin, and Du Fu (2019)
The Correspondence of David Cope and Allen Ginsberg (1976-1996) (2021)

Anthologies (as editor)

Nada Poems 17 peers (1988)
Sunflowers & Locomotives: Songs for Allen (1998)
Song of the Owashtanong: Grand Rapids Poetry in the 21ˢᵗ Century (2013)

Editor and Publisher

Nada Press *Big Scream.* 60 issues (1974-2021).

Online

Search for The David Cope Papers
at the University of Michigan Special Collections Resource Center

Foreword

Compassion and awareness, the heart spoke first, and I set my stamp of approval there, but I have also pursued the ambiguities, the multiple layers of conflicting experience, the paradoxes that force us, blind and deaf, to grope our way without the pat assurances of those so certain they've found their way—to move through the darkness of time and retrieve the complexities of vision beyond what machine mentalities with their continuous barrage of debased language, simplistic answers, slogans, political and commercial hounding would program us to ignore, and to play, to strut sweetly with the uncertainties, to dance among the paradoxes.

If the poem rings the bells in someone's clouds, so much am I the happier, yet I would also play and turn the wheel. My writing began with what Allen Ginsberg identified as the "tradition of lucid grounded sane objectivism . . . following the visually solid practice of Charles Reznikoff and William Carlos Williams," and while that visual aspect—attentiveness to what Blake called "minute particulars"—has been important to me, my books have developed as a series of experiments constructing interlocking suites using a variety of images as connecting motifs, continuing series (the love poems for Sue, the kayaking adventures on Michigan rivers, mountain climbing and descent into Haleakala caldera, garden work and eco-poems, the poems of war, etc.) and the use of allusions developing intertextual matrix.

I have also deliberately approached style and technique with the idea of maximizing variety, not only continuing the objectivist "postcard" series derivative of Reznikoff and Cendrars, but also developing Kerouacian jazz solo pieces, my own idiosyncratic variations of middle eastern ghazals, funky sonnets, dialect testimonies and dramatic monologues involving voices overheard in lunchrooms and on dark streets, vers libre tercets loosely based on the dantescan model, dream and visionary poems scribbled out of sleep, spatial explorations after WCW's late models, multi-stanzaed poems set up as an Aleutian chain of stanzas in a sea of silences, Whitmanic prophetic chants and quietly Berriganlike personal poems.

I am interested in a multi-dimensional language which is both plain and elegant: accessible to those with no knowledge of traditions yet also a feast of techniques and allusions for those with greater knowledge, neither reader barred from the poem. Each poem requires attentiveness to shape and sound. It requires groundwork, sweat; it must be earned and is not a given. One must also "go back to the people" because the poem that is disconnected from human *need* has no depth or sustenance for those who come to it, as Williams noted. This book is my final statement and here I rest, content, hopeful that even the darkness of this time must pass.

I salute five friends most responsible for guiding me through my career: poet and guide, Robert Hayden, who taught me to write what matters and to give it refined critical attention in revision; my wife Suzanne, who stood by me through the many turns of a long marriage, always reminding me to follow my star; Allen Ginsberg, dear friend and mentor over 26 years of working together with the gift of poetry and the importance of poetic communities and friendships; longtime companion and brother poet, Jim Cohn, whose journey through the years has paralleled mine as we continuously opened ourselves to each other; and Professor Zhang Ziqing, who translated my poems and published them in China, followed not only the beats and postbeat poets to make their works available for Chinese poets and scholars, and who is responsible for my life-changing journey to China in 2019.

Thanks too to Anne Waldman, Andy Clausen, Antler, Jeff Poniewaz, James Ruggia, Peter Hale, Bob Rixon, Bob Rosenthal, Marc Olmsted, Michael Pingarron, Eliot Katz, Danny Shot, M.L. Liebler, Fin and George Drury, George Drury Jr., Michael Schumacher, Bill Morgan, Zilka Joseph, Nancy Mercado, Wang Ping, Carmen Bugan, Maria Mazziotti Gillan, Katie Kalisz, Joy Gaines-Friedler, Barbara Saunier, Maria Arrieta, Melissa Wray, Keli Masten, Christine Stephens-Krieger, Scott Krieger, Jon Dambacher, Mursalata Muhammad, Usha Akella, Gordon Ball, Kirpal Gordon, GF Korreck, Dave Roskos, David Kuebeck, Eric Greinke, and for the memory of Allen Ginsberg and my first publisher, Tom Lanigan.

—David Cope

Contents

The Rain: Early & Restored Poems 1971-1983

Refugees	3
American Dream: The Fall of Saigon	4
Lamentations	5
Reliving the News	6
Washington	7
Up All Night	8
The Rain	9
The Exchange	10
Operating Instructions	11
Monday Morning	12
On the Road	13
Paterson Falls	14
Roses	15
Euclid Avenue	16
Waiting for The Clash	17
Dreaming on You	18
Seven a.m. Buffing the Floor	19
Among Daisies & Lily Blossoms	20
Quitting Time	21
Train Crossing	22

Quiet Lives 1975-1983

American Dream	25
Abandoned Hotel	26
A Quiet Life	27
The Welfare Office	28
Tears	29
The Shotgun	30
Empty Street	31
End of the Shift	32
Paint Work	33

The Landlady   34
The Plumber   35
Peace   36
A View from the Road   38
A Million Mute Corpses Speak   39
Burning Babies   40
The Odor of Death   41
Slagboom Tool & Die   42
CETA Office   43
Crash   44
Lunch Hour   45
Turning   46
Chinese Calligraphy   48
Rexroth Gone   49
Baseball   50
Labor Day   51
The First Death   52
Sweeping   54
May   54

On the Bridge 1983-1986

Party Talk   57
Modern Art   58
Antietam   59
The Liberty Bell   60
CIA Manual Discovered   61
Cricket   61
Alone   62
Blue April   63
At the Croyden   64
Old Woman in the Café Window   65
"Take Care of Yourself"   66
Landlady on the Stoop   67
The Breakwater   68
Further Progress   69
The Old Stebbens Place   70
Taylor Bridge to Pines Point   71

Sears Service Center Waiting Room   72
Midwinter Cleanup   73
New Windows   74
Getting the Pump Out   75
The Flood   76
Mottled Wings   77
Easter   78
Rhubarb   79
Catch   80
My Father   81
The Lights of St. Ignace   82
On the Main Road   83
Memorial Stone   84
Soft Rain   85
Moonlight & Sunrise   86

Fragments from the Stars 1986-1990

Industrial Clinic   89
The Invisible Keys   90
Blowout in Fast Traffic   92
Hot Coals Burning on Your Tongue   93
Tiananmen Square Sequence   94
Iran   96
On Ramp at Rush Hour   97
Rainy Dawn   98
The New Foot   99
Alex Jane   100
New Moon   102
For Suzanne   104
Will   105
Albeniz, Sor, & Sanz   106
Sleep   107
Old Man   108
Killings to be Made in Soy Bean Futures 109
For Billy   110

Before I Leave for the Mountains   111
Gone West   112
Chorus of Snores   113
Diné Woman   114
July   115
Harvest Sundown   116
Sundown   118
After the Long Hard Day   119

Coming Home 1990-1993

The Return   123
Armstrong to Gothics   124
Coming Home   126
Fireball in the Clouds   127
In Fitful Sleep   129
Below the Headlines   130
The Front Lines   131
Ghazal for the Coming Spring   132
Words   133
Sunday Morning   134
Pointing It Up   135
AP Wire Story: "Janitors at Risk"   136
The Abandoned   137
Pacific Sundown   138
Sierra Madre & North to Oregon   139
Audubon in Fog: The Descent   140
A March Blessing   142
Catching Nothing   143
For Helen Cope   146
Midsummer Night   147
The Abandoned City   148
Convent Garden   149
For Fin & George   150
Farewell   151
The River   152

White Light 153
In Heavy Clouds, In Cold Rain 154
March 155
For All Lost Love 156
"What Thou Lovest Well" 157
Each Wound Became a Voodoo Mouth 158
El Mozote 159
Poem Beginning with a Line by Pound 160
For the Old Man's Tears 161
Ghost Dance for *La Grand Vitesse* 162
A Prophecy 165
The Lovers Sleep 166
Satie & Dante 167
A Charm 168

Silences for Love 1993-1998

The Rhododendron 171
Alba: The Sailors 172
Two Women Dream Together 173
for allen 174
sirens & flashing lights stop 176
The Cranes 177
Two Hearted River 178
He took a long pull on the stout, thanked us all 180
In the Alley 181
The Job 182
Thru Gary & Calumet to the Monet 183
push off 184
Memory in Love 186
Many Reunions 187
New Life 188
A Vision in Manistique 189
The Mirror of Heaven 190
leaving classes 191
the hidden meadow 192

all night   194
For Martin King   195
Turning   196
no time to feel   197
April   198
Free Clothes   199

Turn the Wheel 1998-2003

Lost Loves   203
Fran   204
Solihull to Marylebone   206
Reading the Signs   207
Ghazal of the High Plateau   208
Tender Petals for Calm Crossing   210
The dharma at last   212
ER Saturday Night   214
In Silence   215
Blue Notes for New York   216
Ground Zero   217
Bomb Fragments, Body Parts,   218
The Disappearing Sages   219
The Gift   220
Gone (as you are)   221
Owashtanong Sunrise   222
The white-bristled sallow face in the photo 224
After Ronsard   225
The Fourth   226
In a Sentimental Mood   227
Canyon Rim to Hopi Point Sunrise   228
Lear by Lanternlight   229
Yeah, an' here he was,   230
"La Goulue" Considers His Lines   232
Madadayo in Dreams   234
Out thru the eye beyond the stars   236

The Night Blooming Cereus 2003-2007

The Night Blooming Cereus	239
Masks of Six Decades	240
To the edge and back: the gift	241
New Home	242
Hostas	243
Abu Ghraib	244
After Lope	245
Haditha	246
Desert Serenade	247
Marines with Cobbled Armor	248
October Surprise: An Absurd Reverie	249
Rush Hour in the Swamp, Near Hopewell Mounds	250
May	251
Last of My Singing Fathers	252
A Midnight Rose for Michael Pingarron	254
Big Sale Shop, Bargains Galore	255
The City in Agony	256
Seul Choix Shoreline, Owashtanong Dreams	257

Frail Dreams 2008

Frail Dreams: a suite for my mother 1923-2008

As My Mother Lay Waiting	261
Starlight Call	262
Fallen	263
Death, You Come	264
Frail Dreams	266
The black bees	267
Between Sleep & Wake	268
Her New Room	269
Mais où sont les neiges d'antan?	270
Last Look	271
A Dream of Jerusalem	272
Crystal Lake to Beulah	274

Flight to Phoenix: a suite for my father 1920-2008

The Swimmer   276
Flight to Phoenix   277
In My Father's House   278
The Empty Chair   279
Tahquamenon   280
River Rouge   281
Happy Birthday: you'd be 99   285

September Moon 2009-2013

Andrey Voznesensky   289
Emile at the Crossroads   290
March   291
She   292
April   294
The Crippled Doe   295
Two for Creeley   296
Blues for Frank   298
American Pewter with Burroughs II   300
For Antler, After the Storm   301
Thornapple   302
So the day begins   303

The Gateless Gate 2014-2016

I, You, She or He   307
A Language of Our Time   308
Wyrd Song   311
Early Spring Morn Milwaukee   312
Adieu à Jeff Because   314
Dawn Kayaking the Owashtanong   315
Rix is Gone   318
End at the Beginning   319
The Gateless Gate   320
May Song   321

The Work   322
"the weight of the world is love"   323
Leaves in Fall   324
long thin clouds   325
For Anne at 70   326
Minneapolis Airport Delay   328
The Train: *Howl* in Chicago   329

The Blue Room of Dreams 2017-2023

Kali Yuga Super Blue Blood Moon   339
The Mountain: Inauguration 2017   340
Fragile Moves   341
Flight to Paumanok: A Still Station   342
Manhattan from Jersey City   343
After the Polar Vortex   344
The Moon   347
Waiting for dawn in a Beijing hotel room   348
From the top step of Guangde Temple   349
A Song for Our Lady   350
Memory's Balm   351
Beyond the dream, the open door   352
Among the best minds of his generation   353
A Desperate Mother   354
Unbidden Dream: a melancholy evening calm & free 355
Alvin Ailey's Ode   357
Chicago Springtime   358
Silent March Candlelight Vigil for George Floyd 359
Love in the Corona   360
January 6 Suite   361
Onward, as Creeley used to sign   366
Until Love Is Equal   367
Passing Phantoms   368
Hour of the Ghost Dance   369
Ukraine   370
Sanctuary   372

Birthday Dreams for Andy   373
Spirit Walk Sunset   374

Notes   377

Acknowledgements   437

Index of Titles   441

About David Cope   453

O light beheld as through refracting tears.
Here is the aura of that world
each of us has lost.
Here is the shadow of its joy.

—Robert Hayden

Under the burden
          of solitude,
under the burden
          of dissatisfaction,

          the weight,
the weight we carry
          is love.

—Allen Ginsberg

Early & Restored Poems 1971-1983

Refugees

are like crooked men
                 arrayed
like black ants
         streaming down
              the road,
       raising cloud
pillars in sunlight.

They are dying slowly,
             their backs
forever bent, carrying
          small bundles,
             blackened
cookpots. Mementos
that look like home.

         Their movements,
despite the sun,
     are furtive.
       It is as if
          unseen eyes
watch.

Like grass, like all mankind, they bend
         ever more earthward,
carrying
     garden memories
       and house gods
who did not help.

1971, revised March 2022

American Dream: The Fall of Saigon

the woman heard rockets falling
& rushed into the street with her children
as the whole block went up in flames.

the government wrangles all day,
deposing one president, electing another,
wanting someone acceptable for negotiation.

the American embassy:
marines stand along the walls
smashing the knuckles of South Vietnamese
trying to get in, to be evacuated.

Helicopters rise into the night—
last Americans, rich Vietnamese.
on rooftops & in the streets,
crowds raise their arms in the light of flares.

all about them there is thunder, white flashing,
rumblings throughout the city.

Lamentations

so many jumped out windows
falling like bags of blood

so many nailed to walls
by singing, burning lead

so many fell into this grave
like wheatsacks full of stone

so many point up to a silver glint
& watch their deaths fall to earth

so many tear out their throats
so many have died screaming

the hand like a wing rises again
nailed.

Reliving the News

DMZ:

the sounds enter the ear
like bullets
tearing holes in the brain

the mind collapses
like a bombed wall

the body staggers
goes slack & lies
like a pile of chains

& waking years later
one finds blue smoke

still wafting from
between the lips.

Washington

the politician's smile—
his gestures before the camera—
his hand, waving, as he edges
away from the crowds—

tenements cluster beyond
the white marble pavilions,
broken steps & windows, basketball
in weedy lots crowded with trees of heaven.

now senators look up from the table:
the expressionless eyes,
mouths full of the GRAND SPEECH.

far away, the war goes on,
the heart still pumps gushing blood
out the neck of the headless corpse.

Up All Night

light in the east, red clouds rolling—
leaves shake free, swirling in the wind.

all the faces we've lost—
all our lovers sing to us
out of fields floating in goldenrod.

finally the morning is a dream,
we fall asleep in each other's arms.

The Rain

in memoriam Charles Reznikoff

looking for it, silence is nowhere.
the knifeblade scrapes on the cutting board,
children yell across the meadow.

the sad news reaches me,
this grey morning has made me turn again.
now the rain gusts over the pavement.

another is gone, the old poet whose steely voice
shook compassion from sorrow,
       celebrated the workers' endurance
the delicate heart even in irony.

when I'm full of sadness, the wind comes to me.
where there's sorrow, let me be there.

The Exchange

crowds of grey-suited brokers,
not a hair out of place,
move out of the canyon into the clear
    sunlight of Wall Street.
their steps are firm & measured—
yet they're stopped at the intersection.

the crowd swells into the street:
below the great brass statue of Washington,
a preacher with a straw hat
stands on top of his double-parked
    red Cadillac,
shouting & gesticulating,
Bible in his waving right hand.

brokers check their watches,
young boys rush up the steps, spitting &
howling at the preacher.
    across the street,
a scotsman in kilts plays bagpipes—
the sign near his instrument case asks
for money to get "home to Dundee."

Operating Instructions

After the part
is firmly placed
set the screws to it
fill the tank with oil
this is special oil
don't let it run over

then push this button
the electrodes will sear
a hole clean thru

it's that simple
now repeat

Monday Morning

a woman sobbing on the street
walks rapidly thru the crowd,
stumbling alone around a corner.

monday morning,
the mist keeps falling out of the sky.
a funeral procession,
a traffic jam,
a man handing out religious leaflets.

but two old friends appear out of the crowd,
& we're standing in the rain yakking.
still, I've got to go, & going up the hill
wave them good-bye,
turning to see faces on a city bus
staring blankly into the misty city.

On the Road

for Bob Rixon

grey colossus of concrete,
cars whipping thru intersections—
drivers intent on
the bumper ahead, brake lights, rear view mirror,
merging traffic, horns,
semis raging by in the next lane over—
jam that brake!
a dead stop, sun beating down . . . creep forward . . .
look! four kids beside their car,
steam rising from the hood—
they lift their beers to the driven throng!

Paterson Falls

Roar of the falls across the park:
bright day, Williams' ball players

still race around the bases
gasping in their race for home—

locals too: he also gasping for breath,
big belly, dark skin, dark hair—

& she, hair pinned back, olive eyes,
embroidered smock, watch their boy

stagger thru the grass. Grandmother,
red braid trim, pendant shawl,

watches the three—her old eyes
take in the child's every move.

June 1982, revised June 6 2022

Roses

she fills a pitcher with warm water,
arranges the roses, & does not speak.

when the roses are wilted,
she gathers the dark petals
& mixes them with cinnamon.

I touch the stems,
the dried wounds, the fragrant earth.

she waits by the spring,
looking into the clear water.

Euclid Avenue

At Fat Boy's outdoor barbecue, a girl turns
ribs & chicken among car horns & fumes.

The Health Museum features Juno,
the transparent woman. Crazed boys race

across the street, dodging madhouse traffic,
old heads nod over nursing home balconies.

Troubles? Call a friend—Police Patrolman's Assn.
MUD WRESTLING! Showgirls in the mud.

Near the Terminal Tower Lake Erie shines, distant
as a dream. WMMS—World Series of Rock.

SCREWY LOUIE'S T-SHIRTS. Movies:
THE WOMEN IN CELL BLOCK 7,

MEAN FRANK & CRAZY TONY,
FRENCH FANTASIES, rated XXX.

Now the cop with his gun sidles up
to a parked car, driver slumped in his seat.

Flowers say everything best.

Waiting for The Clash

Boa wrapped around her neck,
she only has eyes for the crowd;

her boyfriend fondles his snake
& kisses it. Near them, new shirts

carefully sliced with razor blades,
safety pin clips clamped onto cheeks

as if they'd really pushed the needles
thru—& bottles! Smashed on a wall

as the crowd pushes thru doors,
revolution? Flying glass in Suzy's eye!

Dreaming on You

for Todd & Don MacIntyre

Another & yet another:
lovers of the sea & sky.
Wherever you go, let it be light.
Stars over dark water,
The moon in tossing leaves.

All our days pass before us,
a string of lights we carry away.
Some to sing & fish in moonlight,
some to dance & shout at the stars,
some to love, some to weep.

Now you go the secret way,
the golden river behind you.
Snow all about me, spring soon.
You're far away from me now,
So I'm dreaming on you.

Seven a.m.: Buffing the Floor

looking up, a boy's at the door,
blood streaming thru his hands,
scalp laid open—numbchucks.
no, he didn't know who did it.
      on the nurse's bed,
      coldpack on his head . . .
he had to get out of there,
staggered to the door
didn't want to talk to no cops.

Among Daisies & Lily Blossoms

my neighbor stands before me.
every siren
is his boy; every wreck on the road
is that mustang cut in half.
even best friends don't know
how to talk about it, stammer or stare.
his wife, seven weeks later,
slams doors, wrings her hands.
but the boy—
the father sighs—he's free of it.

Quitting Time

the field of clover & lace
browns in the heat,

endless plumes of smoke
rising from the factory.

across the parking lot,
a faint moaning sax

pierces the day from
someone's radio.

men rush for their cars—
tense & exhausted,

eyes ringed with sweat.
lunchpails tossed in

back seats, windows down—
punch it for the gate,

off in a roar of smoke
& screaming tires.

Train Crossing

shall I go yea-saying
in the American night?

lights go out in homes
across the continent,

sheets, pillows, hands & hips.
the railroad bell clangs

& horns blare, oncoming
wheels clacking, a red light

down the line where
the track curves in the mist.

Quiet Lives 1975-1983

American Dream

the house was all in flames,
orange billows bursting up into the sunlight.
FBI agents & police were laid up
behind walls, sheds & other buildings
armed with M-16s & rocket launchers.
the firemen were kept back.
the battle had gone on for some time
when the fire exploded thruout the house.
one of the bodies could be seen inside the house,
loaded with ammunition belts,
the bullets exploding from the heat.

Abandoned Hotel

urine, fresh in the doorway,
puddles on the sidewalk.
we key the lock of the abandoned Hillside,
looking for free furniture:
windows broken out, smashed chairs & dressers,
yellowed mattresses laid on the floors,
a Bible, a picture of "Smiling Rose,"
"pussy" sprayed on the wall six times,
& eleven pigeons parading in the hall.
the paint peels from every wall.
outside, a crone wheels a battered pram, empty;
the police have an old man against a wall.

A Quiet Life

Minh will turn down citizenship;
he wants to go home.
the Texans treated him badly
when all he wanted was work, a quiet life.
could we get Sang's children out
in a month or two?
no, said Tham. a time of storms.
on my boat, Lien said, my children go 3 days
no food, & water only to wet the lips.
four people die,
& this in good weather.

The Welfare Office

a fat black woman bellows
at the face behind the desk,
her coat billowing about her boy,
who clutches her knees.
rows of haggard faces wait
in a stupor.
the bureaucrats take them one by one.
forms & signatures, in a cubicle,
muffled conversations,
mechanical clacking.
"drove buses Saigon to Hanoi 2 years?
small appliance repair?
he's lucky, should be no problem
once he learns English."
outside, bodies crowd the lightpoles;
the police lift a derelict
from a boarded doorway.

Tears

a woman sits on the bench
running her hands thru her hair,
sobbing.
snow falls among the graves about her,
she gets up, walks in a tight circle
& rubs her eyes.
the streetlights go on
as her hair fills with snow.

The Shotgun

back from the army,
he went out with friends
& hit the bars.
where'd he been? up to see that bitch? what bitch?
goddamn it, you know what bitch!
the screaming—
out of the closet—he put the slug in—
shut up! I'll kill you,
you keep screamin'—damn bitch!
the police at the door,
a hole in the ceiling,
& she, in the corner, her wild eyes.

Empty Street

the yellow flashers point away to the left;
an empty street,
a vacant lot with steps leading up to nowhere.
the sumacs are lush & tall.
up the hill, old hotels,
grey unpainted buildings with rooms to rent
line the unseen avenue
where broken men shuffle away their days,
& above, the sunset breaks thru clouds,
scarlet lining the broken surfaces of grey.
the wind blows old papers down the street;
his hair flying,
an old man leans against a No Parking sign,
grinning, no teeth.

End of the Shift

women stream out of the factory
swearing down the boss & the union.
the shift is over, the long day,
& though it's a bright afternoon they hardly notice.
they gossip & argue, worrying about traffic.
when they get to their cars
they find them vandalized, here a battery stolen,
here a windshield smashed out,
here the tires taken off, the radio ripped out.

Paint Work

his workmen stopped to listen;
the neighbors opened the window.
he waved his arms
& pointed to the new roof. his expenses:
she hadn't paid in two months.
he hadn't agreed to her painting the place.
where was the contract? show it.
he looked indoors. the chisels began again.

The Landlady

a thousand dead roaches in the sink
& on the floor, a thousand more, crawling.
she wanted "to do business fairly,"
but didn't know whom to trust.
the tenants had tried to set the house afire,
then left, six months back on the rent.
she wonders how to fix the battered wall,
the smashed ceiling, the live wire;
how she'll keep her finances straight,
whether her children are growing up right.

The Plumber

a tank commander in the 3rd army,
he remembers
a sniper perched atop a house
pinning the men down.
he lowered his cannon
& "blew that kraut 30 feet in the air."
& no remorse. they were all so ornery
they'd fight with their mothers.
a clear, sunny day in July
37 years later:
children're playing catch on the sidewalk
& 2 young men sit on a wall,
talking tough, to impress their girlfriends.
an old woman hobbles by,
laughing, an endless laugh all to herself.

Peace

Break Room Blues

sitting around a table waiting for the day to end
sore shoulders & jaws firing rifles at boot camp,
the advantages of the M-16,
how a grenade works,
blasting tiny shrapnel in every direction.
Roger relives watching perimeters at night,
calling artillery strikes on anything that moved:
so jumpy
any monkey or snake in the brush might set him off,
he talks of loneliness, staring into the alien night
when everything he loved was far away.
Jerry—fond of guns & tactics—
proudly remembers taking an M-16 off a dead GI;
he'd been issued an M-14
& wanted a better gun. this was how to get one.
Benny talks of piles of bodies,
corpses with arms, heads, legs ripped off,
the twisted faces of the dead,
the stink that filled his nostrils,
a smell he can't forget.
he speaks without passion,
regretting the wasted effort, the needless deaths,
yet he accepts his part in it,
still amazed people could live like this for years,
from attack to counter-attack
hiding in fields & ditches,
finding uncles & sons blasted to pieces
more often than children are born.

Ann Arbor:

after the politicians' lies, the funerals of friends,
the nightly deaths in the evening news,
our rage swelled into riot.
surging around a lone police car
we smashed the windows out, punching the driver's face in.
others ran thru the main streets;
store fronts & bank windows shattered on the pavement.
as the dark night settled in
we blocked traffic, heading farther & farther downtown.
suddenly police filled the streets before us—
gas masks, nightsticks, dogs straining at leashes.
a charge!
shouts! screams! nightsticks cracking skulls!
tear gas all over main street! panic!
some ran blindly, in any direction,
officers in gas masks on their heels;
others sat down in the street, folding their arms,
waiting to be beaten & carried off.
up the dark alley! thru sidestreets, home again,
& once home
I looked at my face in the mirror,
filled with rage & horror, alone & cut off.

years later, on a picnic,
we watch light play thru willow branches.
listening to this soft breeze
I wonder how I put the violence behind me.
so many friends dead
& those come back still dazed & broken,
yet the night passes, somehow.

A View from the Road

rows & rows & rows & rows
identical white stones
in the late afternoon sun.
we pass, in a hurry,
hardly giving them a second thought.
& at the VA Hospital
over the hill, unseen from the road,
those legless & armless men are waiting,
those old screamers
who can't put away the nightmares,
the shell-shocked mutes
drooling in their wheelchairs.

A Million Mute Corpses Speak

when the senators questioned the general
about his former role, he said
the whole nation owes allegiance to the president,
regardless of what he does.
his blue eyes glittered in the cameras.
he shifted in his seat, a smile on his lips.

Burning Babies

Israel, Lebanon, the burning babies,
women raising their hands to the sky
shrieking before pillars of black smoke.
messengers race thru rooms of state
chattering their nothings for the media.
Begin smiles & regrets; Sadat smiles & regrets.
at last the fighting ends.
now come the justifications,
wishing the blood off their hands.

The Odor of Death

after the national guard broke thru the rebel lines,
the Red Cross followed;
they wore gas masks to stifle the odor of death,
collecting the bodies, some days old,
to be burned & buried.
Somoza claimed total victory:
his planes strafed roads into Costa Rica,
stopping the refugees in their tracks,
killing the wounded, the aged, the sick.

Slagboom Tool & Die

Tham is tiny among these burly Americans
shuffling thru the room,
filling out applications.
a man turns to me:
"thirteen months I been lookin'—
no goddamn jobs anywhere, 'less yer a
nigger er Veetnamese—"
a glance at Tham.
a door slams. an angry man pushes past us:
"I want my steward!
they're pushin' us too damn hard!"

CETA Office

the clerk talks as if to himself.
"fled the draft . . .
wife & children left behind . . . "
Sang looks to me,
then back to Lien, who sits, hands folded.
his countrymen are tearing up Kampuchea,
& this new land, so different & strange—
they whisper in Vietnamese.
the clerk looks up.
a job, maybe . . . how long can we wait?

Crash

the cars lie, one on its side,
a rear wheel still spinning,
& the other upside down.
the bodies are scattered across the cornfield,
bent & broken on the frozen ground.
two ambulances pull up.
the attendants arrange & cover the dead.
cars pull over to the side of the road,
everyone shuffles,
eager to help, hands in pockets.

Lunch Hour

waiting for a bus
some laid-off workers shoot craps.
this one's won, he's dancing around
slapping at the losers.

Turning

thin clouds over the treetops,
red dawn on the horizon.
you sleep,
one bare leg extended beyond the covers,
as I get up, scratching my head,
to throw my clothes on & turn the key for work.
how many millions are doing this at this moment?
& how many, scattered across the time zones,
are eating lunch, taking breaks,
turning the screw, loosening the locks?
how many're sound asleep?
I've been asked for a poem on nuclear war—
disarmament—
the faces, city streets & country roads,
turning, turning, turning, thru quiet lives,
only sunrise & sunset certain,
the crowds at Kelvinator's door,
at GM & Reynolds Aluminum each morning,
red eyes, pot bellies, thick hands, lunch pails,
steel-toed boots, whispers, cigarettes,
fingers gesturing;
the crowds at City Hall, secretaries primping
before the window glass
as the janitors unlock the doors,
the men in suits swaggering in with their briefcases,
golf talk, cocktail chatter;
street sweepers, cops, bums waking under
railroad trestles & freeway overpasses,
the crowds at the unemployment office,
the lines at welfare,
farmers hauling in their apples & peaches & corn,
decrepit pickups still making those corners:
in ten thousand cities across the globe.
& still these politicians don't sit down,

still the generals swagger
& the arms makers press for more.
that single flash! that unimaginable heat!
that moment of terror & sickness—
let's keep our love,
let us be tender with one another.
the earth still turns; the days grow shorter;
hazy sun
still quiets the anxious heart;
Walt Whitman,
would you call for hope at this hour?

Chinese Calligraphy

T'ang Yin, Freer Gallery

Dreaming of Immortality in a Thatched Cottage—
a man
surrounded by the immensity of trees, mountains & sky,
dreaming,
& in the sky his other self has left it all behind.
coming in here:
car horns, a small boy tried to strangle a pigeon,
throngs sat in the shade, wiping their brows,
taxis slammed on their brakes.
& I, I would leave this place?

Rexroth Gone

tenderly now,
let me blow this faint gentle breath out
 to another of my fathers.

two days since I heard this news,
& all day today heaving & sighing,
 his mountain meadows, the Spanish dead,

Sacco & Vanzetti, Dylan Thomas,
& all the tiny plum blossoms he floated us:
 if I sit tonight in shadows,

the moon'll be full, the crickets sing
sweet lament. tenderly now,
 this faint gentle breath to you,

Kenneth.

Baseball

the farmboy's proud of his white uniform
with the red trim.
under the white lights
he & others play baseball.
they're dazzling on the green.
a hit!
the crowd stands up, mouths full of popcorn!
the ball goes high over the lights
disappearing over the bushes at the field's edge
into the dark river beyond.

Labor Day

all our jams are up,
our watermelons, tomatoes, cukes & peaches.
cruising past these fields of corn,
their tassels shining in the sundown,
already I'm dreaming of Thanksgiving.
in fall I can't help but think of death,
its dear color:
already here & there the maples turn;
here is a funeral cortege, holding up traffic,
the women covering their faces,
heads bent, the men solemn, staring straight ahead.
a whole life passes before me,
someone I never knew;
the sun shines over the hearse, thru the windows
onto their laps where their hands are folded.

home, sitting on the porch with you,
these sweet short moments
talking & looking over our marigolds
never come often enough.
yet together our lives're kind: we get by,
savoring this time
as the gardener puts his yard in order.
everywhere I look, people are whistling, busy:
now's the time to read Whitman again.

The First Death

Chris was already dead,
the pieces shipped home from DaNang.
childhood friends walked up the hill
in the rain,
remembering campfires & gravel roads,
swimming bare-assed in the river at dawn.
a pump jock,
I worked 3rd shift, had to get used to
drunkards pulling in at 3 a.m.,
their spit & abuse,
rich men,
angry if I didn't get their windows clean,
& blacks, whose eyes spoke only of
The National Guard on their burning streets
the summer before.
I'd rush out of the back room
where Milton or Wittgenstein lay open
among the oil cans:
"yes sir, what can I do for you?"
hands & feet smelling of gasoline,
the river running in my waking dream
at 4 or 5 a.m., the carp spawning
slapping their tails on the rocks at dawn,
the mist rising over the water,
gone with the slightest breeze.
my brains were ground into that pavement,
I found my fellow men
not so kind, & girls'd call me all night long—
"hey honey, how'd 'ja like to check my oil?"
weekends,
I'd hit The Spot, surrounded by
the gruff old men I'd loved years before;
now their sour jokes about "niggers"
turned my stomach.

they'd buy me beer, wanting to fight about
Vietnam & Nixon & hippies,
never giving me a moment's peace.
drunk, I'd wander home
under the swinging street lamps
dreaming of Chris, tears all over my face,
& stop at the dam to watch
the water roaring & foaming,
the full moon overhead,
not knowing what I'd done to find myself
here,
trembling to wake to another day.
who could say to me then,
someone's coming
to show you a way?

Sweeping

two mechanics sit in broken glass,
one cigarette between them
passed back & forth,
taking turns reefing on a stubborn wheel nut.
the poet appears,
broom & dustpan in hand.

May

wasp, how did you find your way
to my windowsill?
sunlight frames your tiny feelers & legs,
your fragile wings.

On the Bridge 1983-1986

Party Talk

over there . . . every day it was life & death . . .
my life . . . so BORING
since I came back . . .
he leaned forward, pointing his finger at me,
knowing I wasn't one of those who faced bullets.
 . . . those gooks . . .
you wouldn't believe what they did
to the American dead!
his fists clenched & unclenched.
I thought of the severed Vietnamese fingers
my friend's brother had sent back in the mail.
there was nothing more to say;
I went to the next room & danced with the girls.

Modern Art

an old bum scratches his back beneath his coat,
staring in the window at the auto parts store;
a sign—MODERN ART—is placed before
a crankshaft standing straight up
mounted on a bell housing,
carburetor & air cleaner for head & hat,
chains hanging down for arms.
the traffic's heavy at this hour. the bum turns away,
leans against a light pole,
pulls out a cigar stump & lights it,
watching the furious drivers curse each other
in the cool, bright morning.

Antietam

horses' tails swish in a sunlit field.
traveling to Antietam, she recalls a war story:
        her father, Uncle Bob said, was
always gentle
& kind, always ready to laugh—
never angry.
her mother remembered other things:
he'd wake up sweating—
wild eyes in the night—
the German officer he had to shoot, point blank—
those eyes, that cringe,
night after night.

        in the cornfield
where the blue boys lurched & shrieked,
the cannons're set up as in the old photograph,
but freshly painted, with an asphalt walkway curving around.
& in Bloody Lane,
where bodies were heaped up waist-high,
I marveled at bees in the corn tassels not 30 feet away.
at Burnsides Bridge, the lazy river barely rippled.

23,000 killed, wounded & missing here.
"such a
beautiful vista," the old man said, leaning on his cane:
fields spread out
for miles, lines of trees & hills,
farmers on tractors,
eyes back & down to the turning discs,
or pulling tanks,
insecticide hissing over the fields:
"not a cloud in the sky."

The Liberty Bell

now highlit with spotlights
& once the lecture's done,
they'll let you touch it!
looking the crowd over:
suburban husbands shorts & polo shirts,
expensive cameras on braided straps,
nagging wives, their kids push & press
to run their hands along the rim
& giggle;
Japanese tourists pose with the bell behind,
hands behind back, grinning—
nephew or wife snaps them
again & again;
a Sikh stands near the back of the room,
hands folded together,
eyes intent, lips pressed together.

CIA Manual Discovered

blood is water
& a knife is a vote.

Cricket

how'd you get inside this wall?
you should be out with the flowers.

Alone

        the boss has gone.
stop
& look out the window:
        a big man has come out on his porch
& stretches
in the morning sun, swinging his arms.

                  up the ladder
I take chisel & hammer in hand
& knock out the old plaster—
        delicious
        silence,
 little sharp raps—
& now the neighbor's hanging out his laundry.

Blue April

below the 3rd floor fire-blackened brick
& empty windows, torn curtains hanging,
a young woman,
       rag tied about her hair,
       curls falling at her ears,
waves & calls
to slicked-up goodtime Charley
who's strutting thru the paper scraps,
       giant ring on his pinky finger,
       black & white tu-tones shining.
           he stops
& tilts his hat, gazes above, shakes his head
& turns,
heading thru the garbage cans
to the door leading to her darkened stairs.

At the Croyden

smell of fish frying thru an open door
& up the stairs
a fat woman in a floral dress bright orange & red
screams in the stairway
at anyone who'll listen,
young dude leaning against
 a doorway nearby
picking his teeth, spitting big gobs on the floor.
 another door opens:
an old man, bent but with a bright eye.
seeing me, a stranger, with my mop bucket & Stones T-shirt,
he wonders, d'you own the building? no?
you like music? he used to play—jazz, supper clubs,
& he was happily married, too, bless her,
she passed on. dropped dead right in the living room,
just the other side of this door.
he played everywhere, all these big joints downtown,
an' he played Detroit, & up in Canada, too.
he knew all the good numbers—
didn't play much now, no money for a piano.
 his breath, alcohol, leaning into me as he speaks—
the woman who'd been screaming passes by now,
shades over her eyes—
"don't listen to him, damn fool talk yer arm off
& none of it don't mean shit!"
he looks at his hands, palms down, fingers spread,
& looks back up into my eyes
 & I see the invisible keys.

Old Woman in the Café Window

the old woman sits alone & dreams at her table,
stirring her coffee, gazing thru the window
as crowds of office workers push thru the door,
shaking their boots off, talking the latest news,
elbowing their way to the milks in rows,
the coffee machine, the cook who looks up expectantly,
potatoes & scrambled eggs, sausages & bacon in heaps
steaming before him.
she watches them, absently, as they pass,
then turns again to the window,
her right hand patting stray strands of silver hair
into place behind her ear,
her rubber boots placed neatly beside the empty chair
across from her, now she has opened her purse,
& is looking into a tiny compact mirror.

"Take Care of Yourself"

are you kidding? do I look like
     the kinda guy who'd get attacked?
hands to his breast,
huge belly, shining eyes.
then, as we were passing out of the park,
cupping his hands to his mouth,
ya-ha! that's what Jesus said
     before they nailed him up!
his big hand waving,
we disappear in the rush hour crowd.

Landlady on the Stoop

sittin' right here, I got robbed—2 weeks ago.
high shrill voice.
her old man got out of his car,
brought her the cigarettes & sat down.
salsa in the street.
    she continued:
a man appeared before her,
leaned up—as if to whisper something—
& ripped her necklace from her chest.
it was just cheap costume jewelry!
glance at the neighbors
chatting in the windows above us—
they know who did it, but they won't tell.

The Breakwater

for my father

red dawnlight on the white & red checked tablecloth,
cool air deep in the lungs:

     so seldom

we were together.
thru the sand, to the breakwater:

      how big the perch were!

the shouts of men & boys,
hauling them in over & over, the lines flying out,
cranking reels, & pails filled with flapping tails.

Further Progress

for Nate Butler, shot in the head

the eyes wide open, glaring,
head surrounded, an aura of tubes
taped to his forehead,
his beard curled over the sheet. I read him
Williams' *Red Lily*: tumbling daisies
one by one—softly. he grunted, yes, yes,
his eyes closed, & he was asleep.
I rose to leave, he woke again:
I laid my fingers tenderly on his forehead.

The Old Stebbens Place

house & barn long fallen in
foundation cracked
wild grape & maple growing
thru the rotted timbers
moldering where the basement was:
maybe the father was
called out & killed in war,
or they couldn't keep it—
crop failure; maybe
they just left,
let it go, lost their sense of place
& moved on.
we stood a moment & dreamed their dream,.
water rippling in the nearby stream

Taylor Bridge to Pines Point

take the canoe thru rocks shoals a
    sharp bend,
            another,
 watch out for that
dead tree
hanging in your face,
 keep your
 eye on those
 white waves ahead.

now a delicate, gaudy
great blue heron
lifts off ahead
    & slowly flaps
    its way aloft
where it finally soars
over the treetops,
         gone.

after the trip,
sleep all afternoon.
    the fire goes out
& all the boys arrive, run away
to the river,
board their canoes & disappear
    around the bend,
laughing & hallooing.

at night, a thousand stars.
across the clearing,
the lantern's shine,
the branches, still, above.

Sears Service Center Waiting Room

the flower-strewn corpse of Indira Gandhi:
her eldest son, now prime minister,
calmly lays the torch at her side.
relatives pile the wood around her—
seen on TV
in this waiting room, heard over intercom jabber.
a girl stands at the glass door, anxious,
looking out as mechanics strip the nuts from a wheel;
an old man wonders whether the wait's too long—
maybe he should call off his deal
for a new battery
now.

Midwinter Cleanup

he & the boss argued
how many rooms & how to do 'em & how'd they ever get
that much done;
the rest of the crew leaned against the walls
& perched on the stairs, watching the falling snow outside.
as a kid, he & his brother
walked the tracks with wagons & picked
the coal that'd flown from the coal car
when the tenders were pitching hard;
or they brought laundry from the "richies"
for their mother to do
& pumped the outside well for water to fill the tubs
so she could wash—
sometimes the "richies" wouldn't pay, saying
the sheets weren't clean enough.
when the war came, he enlisted,
went to Bougainville, saw little action but recalled
a marine whose buddies had all been tortured to death
ordering the guards aside so he could
blast 8 Japanese prisoners;
& he could still see
the freed Americans whose faces had the twitches
& the fingers destroyed with bamboo stakes.
finally, the boss walked out,
& he followed, shaking his head,
his watery eyes cast down.
he stopped, explained the boss's ideas to the crew,
& sighed: "a few months more, & I can forget it all."

New Windows

in the grey shadowy basement workroom
the landlord brought me the windows
& I heated the old putty with a torch & scraped it out,
nicking out the push points & pulling the broken glass.
 the inspector had ordered it
 & would be back Monday.
a quiet moment,
listening as the old building creaked above:
two on the stairs
talking about the grocery bill as they went up;
in one apartment,
kids racing around shouting, bouncing a ball,
& now, directly above me,
a gospel tune on the record player,
ladies in the kitchen shouting along with the singer
& clapping, clapping, clapping their hands!
 I laid the new windows in place
& stretched & rolled the new putty, firmed it up
& pressed & slid the knife along, a clean line!
& turned the frame & began again.

Getting The Pump Out

the valves're closed;
the gushing stops.
blue-white light from the welder's torch
strobes the well pit:
finished at last, he clambers out.
sledges hammer the old pipes loose;
the men hold their backs & stretch between blows.
the pipe-fitter balances over the pit,
his legs spread, bending to
hook chains to the cast-iron block;
the hi-lo forks rise,
the chains go taut—
swinging, the heavy pump appears above the pit.
the workers stand & watch,
wiping their hands on their blackened bellies;
foreman behind them
tugs on his cigarette,
his shiny red pants sagging over his heels.

The Flood

a canoeist who challenged this current
fell in & was swept away—
ancient Indian Mounds themselves now islands—
a whole woods underwater:
little crests rise against the big trees & part,
the water swirling around & rippling below,
branches & sticks & ice chunks jammed up
against fallen trees or between 2 or 3 trees standing,
& out in the main current,
giant ice floes flotsam of old docks & broken boats,
uprooted bushes & tree trunks
race in the wild water, jostling,
crashing against bridge pylons,
swirling away around the bend.
cars stop along the old park road,
drivers pausing to watch, eyes wide, hands at lips.

Mottled Wings

stretched
to catch
the headwinds, a huge hawk

soars,

turns, adjusts

to quick new

gusts,

plummets

downward then
catches another cross current to
keep his place, his eyes ever below
where the canoeists,
lost in a dream of ancient cedars,

roots & lichens,

the timeless river,

look up, pointing thru the morning sun
to see the acrobatic
struggle above,

small prey along the banks
hidden from deadly view.

Easter

another day of work.
too many days of work.
waiting on the porch with buckets & tools,
look!
a little black girl in the house across the street,
her hand at first shielding her eyes
in the bright morning sunlight,
& then, seeing me, waving a moment—
curtains move, & she's gone.

Rhubarb

the front room full of women,
the nurse giving her instructions—
the fan swiveled back & forth,
they wiped their brows continually.
in the back room she lay gasping,
tongue flopping to one side,
coated with glycerin to keep it from drying.
the women were going in & out,
bathing & powdering her,
changing the sheets when she soiled them.
he sat in the front room & watched,
his face red with the strain.
seeing me, he said, come out in the garden,
I've got some rhubarb for you.
we walked among the beets & peppers & tomatoes.
he took out his knife & began pulling & trimming,
now & then silently looking to me.

Catch

struggle with the fish,
reeling, guiding the line
away from the sunken log—

naked blue lady on his bicep
wiggling as he flexes & relaxes;
high black pompadour glistens,

not a hair out of place.
& now the fish brought to net,
a fine trout, flapping & wiggling:

he yells back to his sleepy boy,
throw a few more on the fire
& grease that pan, we got one!

My Father

standing before the calendar pin-up,
those juicy nipples, that tongue on the lip,
he explains new ways to get the work done better.
& there, at the mouth of the blast furnace—
his hand stretches out to survey a black man in blue
furiously checking parts,
blowing off a die, pushing the next button
to slam the dies together & pump the molten metal in,
shouts in the roar of fans & motors.
I grew up watching him from afar;
for years we fought, if silently.
dumbfounded before my first struggling poems,
he defended them to my aunt, who complained
they'd make me no money, & ruin my life.

The Lights of St. Ignace

heavy slapping rain over their heads—
windshriek thru the cedars along the shore,
whitecaps row on row, thundering against the beach,
visible even in the dark:
                    she lay on her back, looking up
as the tent poles bent farther & farther down,
each gust slamming the canvas closer to the ground.
he fought his way from corner to corner outside,
pushing the stakes back in place, adjusting guy lines,
the wind whipping his coat loose around his waist.
far out, the searchlight on the island
lit the clouds in its turning circle,
& to the right, across the long bay,
the lights of St. Ignace shone peaceful as a quiet day.

On the Main Road

the great flare of a burning tanker
shoots up white-yellow into the deep night,
the smoke black even against the sky.
      figures of men lean on bumpers,
stand in headlights, gesturing
in the great light ahead;
        distant,
police & ambulance race out of the city,
white lines flying beneath them.
      I see it all from afar,
on another road.
my turn-off comes:
unlock the doors, get the lights on,
make coffee & await the administrators,
say hello to all the perfumed ladies
& ambitious young men
racing to make the grade.
      on the news, 9 o'clock:
the driver lived, pulled from the wreck
moments before the whole tank blew.

Memorial Stone

a young man kneels on a stoop in the alley
& blows trumpet,
soft sad notes rise into the breeze;
                  a block down, beyond the shadows,
cabs & trucks & old Chevys roar in a spot of sun.

my hand, against the memorial stone, again
traces friends dead in war.
I sit—& watch the bag ladies & pigeons passing,
the water's shine as it rises from the fountain,
the manic ex-soldier who goose-steps back & forth.
              the faces rise again in my mind:
blond hair cut straight across,
his raised hand & shouted hello along the river
on a home-made raft;
                      & the other, all curls,
his Latin books shoved in a corner,
V-8 engine pulled apart in his bedroom,
smiling in his grease-marked underwear.

            jostled now—
            "you po-lice?"
he asks, then "hell, no, not widdem clothes on!"
his eyes on my janitor uniform—
reaches into his pocket for his bottle
& offers me a slug of sweet red wine,
motorcycle cap backwards on his thinning pate.
         we sit together, saying little,
          glad for quiet company.

Soft Rain

window with
jagged hole

dark living room
a table lamp

barely visible
& a woman's arms

the hands
calmly knitting—

but here
on the porch

a small boy's
skipping

watching himself
skip

in the door glass
as the rain

softly falls
into the grass

Moonlight & Sunrise

half-moon shines thru
mist & silvered clouds,

over the beaded lawn,
the dewy junipers.

you turn in sleep,
tiny child grows within

as I kiss you lightly,
sigh, & turn to leave.

turn the key
& wipe my brow,

get to the doors I'd open.
pass the silent aspens,

the oaks & dogwoods,
swamp pools reflecting

sky & moon, pass
the Indian Mounds,

sleeping bones
we'll all become,

tickled by roots
in eternity. already

the first red clouds
streak the sky.

Fragments from the Stars 1986-1990

Industrial Clinic

the man on crutches,
 leg muscles ripped pushing a heavy load—
the woman, teeth clenched,
hand curling & twitching, too many hours
 polishing pins—
the grandfather, wrist bound into a stump
 where his hand once was—
the woman, barely more than a girl,
 her foot a gauze ball, flesh pierced
 a week before by a punching ram—
all look up
as a dust-covered boy in hard hat comes in
wringing his hands, swinging
his arm & groaning, blood spraying out
 across the floor—
the nurses meet him there & usher him quickly
to a room where the doctor's waiting.
here comes the janitor with his mop.
someone sighs. their eyes follow the mop.

The Invisible Keys

dead, old John, premiere piano player,
found sitting up on his toilet after
3 days not answering his bell:
yellowing sheet music, old records,
unpaid bills
piled on his dresser;
clock radio blaring the latest hits,
the morning news;
government checks stuffed in the mailbox,
unclaimed;
no relatives, no claims for his things,
landlord to arrange his funeral.

spot on
the sax,
he's on his knees making that thing
scream
just above the heads of the dancers
who're humping it,
sea of heads jumping in the dark,
smoke haze up in the lights &
            now it's John's turn,
bass thumping
raw nerves underground raging river,
            he lights into those
high keys, staccato—
fingers flying faster & faster,
sweat dripping off his eyebrows,
crashing cymbal & snares & high hat
            clanging!
& now that guitar coming in
sweet & low,
trying to *take it*—

even the bouncers at the door look in,
            the dancers
stop dead to watch or
collapse into their seats, exhausted,
take it babe—

that guitar

out front all alone
burning away sadness & anger, unpaid bills
& careless loves,
burning a bright new fire
to get them all to that coming dawn,
burning all desire
        away,
leaving them
quiet,
        breathing
 softly
 together
at last.

 Somewhere that old tune's floating up
 in a dingy hallway
one bare bulb hanging
 & those keys're
rolling, waves under fast fingers—
 & two floors up
a woman sobs alone on rumpled sheets
 shattered glass
on the floor, picture on her pillow—
 two lovers
in white, with a red rose—

 hearing those notes
again, she'll rise & look out at
 the empty street,
streetlights going off in the
 lavender dawn,
& she'll remember an embrace, a
 tender moment
in a room like this, & sighing,
 wipe her eyes
& fix her hair, who knows who
 might turn up today,
toes still tapping to that old song.

Blowout in Fast Traffic

limping home
on a beat spare,

bright streetlights
on this deserted street:

the lone pedestrian's
swinging his umbrella.

workers in the old factory
lean across their break table,
laughing, in the window,

as I pass,
far from the fast road now.

the shops're all closed.

moon above,
& faintly,
the scattered stars.

Hot Coals Burning on Your Tongue

in Gaza—
a young woman
raises her hands & tearfully
remembers her sister's last words:
"he killed me!"
—shot dead
by a soldier as she did her laundry.
other relatives
crowd around the woman:
a boy,
his face wrinkled in tears,
the questions still forming, unasked,
his fingers curling
inward to his palms,
& a young man, a brother,
his eyes staring coldly, directly
at you.

Tiananmen Square Sequence

Tiananmen Square

the Chinese student revolt
has sent all the western analysts
scurrying to their Sunday talk shows:

optimistic dreams about Ms. Liberty
whose lamp shines over a polluted harbor
where little men & women race for

more & bigger better lives &
new! improved! ways of making cold
hard cash, avoiding above all any

talk of breath & death.
these students have open eyes.
may they sit, & hear the silence.

Spider Writhing in Lamplight

close the book; turn off the lamp.
you, too, may find light in the dark
& see the thread you hang on.

The Avenue of Eternal Peace

bullets spray; bodies're carried off.
troops advance from east & west
toward the portrait of Mao
where the students man barricades
with rocks & broken bottles.
 we wait, & listen for dispatches
bringing what news can get out:
       once, we too dreamed
we'd sing our way to peace:
brothers, sisters,
I send this slender prayer for you.

The Apology

the lips & cheeks now quiver
in the white light,
in the white room.
the body is bent forward
on a chair, against a wall
facing its accusers:
soldiers with machine guns.
the eyes face the floor.
& now, from the lips & tongue,
abjectly, the apology.

Iran

gas attack:
the bodies
heaped where
they fell, faces
relaxed
in death—eyelashes—
fingers—
lips—
simple white clothes—
a man,
bearded, his head
cradled by rock near
the step
& doorway to
his house—
women & children
fallen together,
their knees—

On Ramp at Rush Hour

April's quick snow melts away:
steam rises from the hot road &
prismic showers
cascade off the exit ramp above

as mad dog commuters
flash thru the falling water
burning up the road

but across
the field among wrecks &
rusted wire bales near where
men used to hop freights
riding the rods
for Chicago & points west—

four men are sitting
around their tiny fire—
warming their hands,
laughing,
slapping their knees,

their camaraderie
as obvious as the sun,
little dog
sitting at the group's edge
motionless.

Rainy Dawn

why think more of living, dying,
this rainy morn, & dream

of all those sleeping friends
& lovers rising now, stretching,

sighing, opening eyes to another
day? pause & remember

the ruined graveyard, the crumbling
walls of the deserted mansion.

the wild rain makes a billion
grassblades jump & tiny rivers roar

giant sandgrains roll past antmound
& sleeping locust & centipede.

the little girl in her fancy dress
parades for her parents,

the old man rocks & reads his paper
& peers thru his rainy window,

invisible sun & stars spin beyond
these clouds & tune our ears

to this fierce rain, shining moment
come to us now.

The New Foot

the door slammed;
cane tapping,

tapping, he works
his way down

the ramp, one hand
against the wall—

men at the table
look up from coffee,

fish stories, tales of
bowling glory.

he stares at the door
20 feet beyond them

where he'll hang his
coat & tool pouch,

then looks down at
his new leg & foot, his

cane, & slowly hobbles
across the room.

heads turned back
to table & talk:

he shuffles
slowly—no more walker,

nor pinned pantleg,
nor therapy, for him.

Alex Jane

under my hand,
moist forehead—
Sue looks up—

the doctors cut
thru flesh wall,
fat layer—

still deeper—
their gloves redden
with her blood—

she is purely
calm, her calm
becoming mine

& now the doctor's
hand enters her
abdomen,

the aide pushes,
pushes,
a blue head appears

wrinkled, angrily
drawing breath—
a howl

as the whole
blue body appears,
cut & clamp,

weigh & check
& suck out nostrils,
hand her to

the father, me,
who sits amazed
as blue flesh turns

slowly pink,
Sue's hand reaching
to touch.

New Moon

tonight
as my baby sleeps

roses & poppies
fill her dream.

new moon,
train whistles

around the bend,
toxic wastes

from Dow
shipped south:

O, the lantern
in the brakeman's hand!

my hair is greying
quickly now;

after barren years
this child's

an unexpected
blessing.

hard to keep
one's mind intact

& calm.
bombers fly above

defending "us."
if we are

breathing here
in twenty years,

what masks
will we wear?

For Suzanne

who'd have guessed
when we watched

the first red dawn
come over the rooftops

of the tenements
together, first night

talking all night, hands
touching & caressing &

bodies warm & softly
moving together,

that years later
I'd be lying here

admiring the curve of
your breasts & back,

the pleasure of your
greying hair, & thrill

still to your hands
touching my shoulders &

caressing my breasts?
O let's be

famous lovers
immortal long after

flesh returns
to earth at last,

Love's example
for those to come.

Will

today, overcast but promising
spring,
        springy step
on the green earth:
 open the door.
 your time is now.

the passage isn't simple
but for those who will
come,
        comes.
                what your father
& mother suffered,
what you suffered,
                is past.

no promises! wake!
                        the heart
has a proper place.
if you'd be clear,
                be calm.
child, young man,
hard laborer,
        sage, old fool,

make it what you will.
will to make it well.

your hands,
for tender touch,

        your ear & eye,
for compassion,

will see & hear
        what's needed:

freely bend your will.

Albeniz, Sor, & Sanz

in the subway, Grand Central:
trains roar in & out,
grateful commuters toss dollars
into the guitarist's case;
they'll shoulder by the moaning derelicts
begging for quarters near the turnstiles,
that monotone chant
halfway to the next world
already—
daylight only two flights up.

Sleep

her small hand curls about the pillow.
the curls of her first hair
bounce back as my hand passes.
I bend & listen to her soft, regular breath
& marvel at lashes, fingernails, lips.

the pregnant woman sleeps as the child within
sleeps,
floating in his bag of waters.
the old man whose death is constant dream
    dreams
sung syllables plunging thru great light
& midnight bell & tender touch—

the battered child in his hospital bed,
the parents who hid their eyes from
    searching cameras,
the cop who kicked the door in—
all sleep, tossing in waves toward another
    shore.

I draw my hand back & look into my daughter's
    sleeping smile;
night & day blur into endless unfolding vision—
& now she wakes, her bright eyes dancing.

Old Man

I saw you lying against a wall
on the ramp to the subway,
your ruddy cheeks
cleft into valleys & faultlines,
your grey beard Whitmanic in dreams,
but matted with dried puke,
your hands
folded across your chest, eyes closed.
I passed you,
knowing you'd be around the next corner, too,
& in the same shape,
nothing to be done.

Killings to Be Made in Soybean Futures

oldtimer swigs & shades his eyes,
look,
my tractor's paid for, but
what a way to end my years farming—
      how many families
      already packing up?
how many men out behind their barns
staring into their own shotgun barrels?
giant dustclouds
roll off his discs & wheels,
last time he'll cultivate these rows,
hopeful shoots
withered in less than a month.
distant heatwaves rise,
distort the hill, the farmhouse,
the line of trees beyond.

For Billy

not so much
what we *want*:
light comes in
passing thought,

in touching hands,
in quiet watching
clouds pass by,
moon in sky—

eyes must open,
mind, be calm.
kind as kin,
this dream!

the end, certain as
a baby's cry:
the babe, the boy,
the strapping man

spring thru a kiss,
matter less than
how we rest
awake in the dream

& see who needs
our touch, our eyes,
& know what can
& can't be done—

light pierces
the raindrop
suspended for its
brief moment,

ornament & complement
to the oak bud's tip.

Before I Leave for the Mountains

Turn him now, she said—
roll
the withered form, bony flanks & buttocks
so she can fit the pad beneath, wash his back,
check for sores, roll him back,
     do the other side,
hook up winch & hoist him tubes & all
     to put a chair beneath
     so he can sit, briefly.

one eye can focus now.
one twitching finger signals yes.
     yet nerves live even in cold limbs.
uncurl his feet, caress them
that he may travel that vast length
of his inert body & reach
his extremities again—
in faltering light, the fire still burns,
steadily, stubbornly:

     only in his own time
     & not in vain.

so the midnight air is cool. walking out,
late & tired, I sigh & sing
     for you.

Gone West

silence above saguaro & cholla—
I stood under the arched vault of the
          ancient cave
& dreamed
where Salado Indians perched & sang—
bringing their corn up from the valley
          singing,
singing by fires that blackened this vault
          forever,
burying their baby among the house walls,
          singing,
sighing, singing in deep night
as the fires flickered lights across the
          ceiling,
singing, standing at the cave mouth
          under the million stars—
vast landscape before my eyes now!
          starshowers! sunrises!
cacti & palo verde over runneled mountains!
          & in the silence,
a low wind, moaning.

Chorus of Snores

12 men in a cabin
    soar peacefully in dreams
12 sets of lungs
    draw breath in & blow out
the successful executive
    blows bullfrog bass,
the long distance bike champion
    turns in short blasts,
the one whose heart is breaking
    is shaking his bed,
     unaware—
the others float soft sighs & snorts
-into the night,
companions & lovers far away
    now above canyon's rim,
worldly dreams & ambitions
afloat in brief eternity—
sigh, brothers,
& moan thru the night,
where the butte's black vastness
is dwarfed by the wild curtain of stars
in your echoing dream.

Diné Woman

silent:
    eyes
follow the white tourists as they
handle the necklaces,
    argue
whether they can afford
this one or that one,
which is better
for whom & whether
it's real turquoise
    or fake.
when they choose,
she slips the trinket into a baggy,
takes the money &, eyes down,
says her thanks.
    now
they're gone.
there is the vast windy silence
    across the land.

July

Anne at fourteen:
                    yellow & peach
roses, daisies, lavenders,
placed
one by one in a slender vase.

rush hour, fumes over the fence:
how many die today,
how many tomorrow?
                    car crash here,
government goon fusillade there,
slow strangling
          by hydrocarbons or
plutonium dust?
a hopeful dream—
peaceful passing in one's bed,
lilacs at the door.

the vase is full,
the last daisy now in place,
& Anne dances
alone in the kitchen,
                    her darkened form
pirouetting with
her invisible partner,
graceful in her abandon.

Harvest Sundown

for Scott MacIntyre

miles of rows
giant rolled haybales

shadowscast
in the stubble where

killdeer killdeer
run on scrawny legs

squawking sirens
humping faked broken wings

as the farmhand
saunters thru, arms akimbo

at his side as if to
ease an aching back—long

day in the field,
sky become merely sky &

this great vista,
with its lines of trees

& rolling land, his
workplace. huge hands

nurture tender shoots
but also kill the dying &

uproot the dead, pasture
gone to scrub 50 years

soon'll be whipped by saw
& bulldozer blade. When he

talks, as he seldom does,
words form from a silence

so intense your ears hurt.
here ravens descend,

great wings over rodents
& scattered seeds

& deer bed down where
the shoeprint line begins.

Sundown

sundown, evening star
over the car lot lights
where the trader waits

over the bridge
where the trucker pauses
& sighs, downshifting,

sundown over the shore,
endless waves
washing in out of nowhere,

gulls flying
to safe harbor,
sundown over the ship

steaming to Chicago,
the sailors pulling their
time on duty,

sundown in the cedar woods
where the silent man
breaks sticks he's gathered

as the small fire leaps again
to light, & the mist
shines about the full moon

quiet in the empty evening,
in the imageless heavens,
quiet, & long sleep.

After the Long Hard Day

half in dreams we lay & held each other
 thru the night.
my hand moved tenderly over your back,
 stroking
 over & over,
our legs intertwined, soft & warm,
& we kissed for a long time,
our hands in each other's hair
as the moon shone thru the windows
filling the room with light.

Coming Home 1990-1993

The Return

the silent winds whirl under condor's wing,
up valleys where bison calves leap
& coyotes prowl, around redwoods &
up concrete canyons, among Wall Street pillars,
past saxophones wailing on 42nd Street,
around the lovers in red-trimmed peasant black
reclining on grass above the sunlit spray
of Paterson Falls, beyond the still-racing
baseball players. millennia pass in falling
water, whole families walk away from homes
where they grew, a woman wipes her eyes
at the edge of her husband's newly dug grave:
many nights I've walked these dreams away,
lovers & friends returning in winds at dawn.

Armstrong to Gothics

the fire's out—tentflap open,
two friends muse & talk:

full moon thru delicate
fingers of hemlock—

orange birch leafclouds beyond,
clinging in a whipping breeze—

even mosses & ferns & barkless
trunks shine in this light,

same stars in ancient Mohawk
dream, same flash of leaves

sailing to earth across
moonstruck land—who knows

where waking ends & dreams begin
as open-eyed sleepers turn?

                up over
       rain & lichen
streaked
      boulders
         thru ripped
up roots &
bleached barkless shattered trunks—
   young balsam firs
poise to push
thru this net of splintered dead
& take the sun.

                taking
rootstump handholds
                        & heaving
our bodies up
                thru giant
splitrock
        crevices among
fern & mossflower,
                        berry brush—
Monarch settles on a fir branch,
airing its wings
as we pass.
        panoramic
redstruck mountains beyond,

                        narrow
        trails
all the way to
        the horizon in mist,
                        wind shrieks
        & whistles
below:
quiet sluff of bootsoles,
        hand to hand
                over the
                        crevasse
        & up the rockface
breathing,
        breathing,
                clear air
        & sky.

Coming Home

lost again in the twilight garden among
fading flowers & the season's last crickets,
I wander among mother's tears & old man's sighs,

the last forlorn embraces of lovers, boys
torn from tender arms & loaded onto trucks
as brass bands blare over camouflaged brims

hiding downcast eyes. tonight, hundreds of
thousands bed down in the desert & hear
their hearts for the first time—cry softly

in the deep night as the moon rises. I pass
thru the now silent garden remembering others,
see the speeches & the firepower arrayed

& the orators on all sides crying *right*—
kingdoms rise & fall & threats become histories
& the agony of thousands fills the wink of an eye.

I turn at last & come home where Sue waits
in the doorway, taking my hand & looking me
eye to eye, the moon risen, full, beyond.

Fireball in the Clouds

the soft snow floats thru
tight-packed buds & flaming
stems. shadows gesture

& talk of ecology. bits of brain,
strands of veins cling to their
words, unseen.

spectres glide in corridors,
   line up at windows & whisper about
     the weather—phones ring,

secretaries coo & yakk—a red mist
   descends & settles over every-
     thing, unseen. protestors

& flag wavers shout in rivers of
   blood & oil that also engulf taxis,
     hydrants, passing buses—

hands raised to flaming clouds,
   a drunken man stumbles & reels
     into the gutter, empty yellow

eyes & open mouth facing fireball heaven.
   peace, peace, a million cry—
     grenades & flags parading from

open mouths. soldiers at briefings
   describe mass murder in surgical
     terms, blue-eyed innocents parade

with flags at the Super Bowl as
   gassed Kurds & blasted Iraqis
     mingle in the silent screams

that rend tender springtime's
           sleeping buds. O fleeting doves,
                       O soft snow, O delicate

curve of wild berry, O sleeping babe
           bombed with dreams, what briefings
                       await you in the nether world?

In Fitful Sleep

legions of bleeding men
drag themselves in line,
armless, blue-black faces
ragged hanging cheeks

& ripped flesh march
with eyes once Johnny's
hanging in their sockets,
march with Bible thumpers

& ancient vets trotting out
flags & angry speeches,
march, young rambos
split from cheek to crotch,

march, arab bashers &
Hussein mashers, march
into the breach, into the
breach—where the god waits

in the center of the fire—
O cringe & tears of mothers
& fathers again, again
anguish of women & young men,

march for oil, march for
flags, march for Hussein,
march for Bush, march for
God, march for right,

march for money, march for
smoke of burning bodies,
 march.

Below the Headlines

below the photo of Cheney & Powell
grinning with a Bart Simpson statuette,

a surgeon in Baghdad amputates
children's legs & arms by candlelight,

no anesthetic; takes blood from one
to give to another, praying the unknown

types are right. the procession continues:
old & young men, bomb-battered women

with babes, faces ripped by shrapnel.
some die for lack of medicine,

clean water, some from the cold night
filled with sirens & bombs & wailing.

The Front Lines

the choices for raw recruits
& boys are simple:

fall back & be shot to death
by the Republican guard

go forward into the mine fields
& be blown to pieces, or

wait for the beefy Americans &
take your chances fighting them.

perhaps the shamal will come early,
then the holy days of Ramadan.

Ghazal for the Coming Spring

broken men march with bleeding ears,
guns trained on their backs, glistening.

here tanks & launchers burned, masses of
corpses flew & fell, ripped & stinking:

here graves mass—open jaws & sockets
of skulls tell no hero's story nor sing

where blood ran into sand & sank,
where rain & shamal remake the land daily:

passing caravans tell & retell a silken
story & pilgrimage sums a lifetime's hope.

women of Kuwait wail & shriek for lost love
& burning wellheads blacken the sky;

across the world, old men dream in
starlit silence among lilacs budding early.

Words

As the Americans stood by,
Saddam bombed Kurds & Shiites—

freedom fighters who dreamed
Bush would stand by his word—

in Turkish mountain camps
children slowly starve.

a Kurdish mother weeps
at her son's open grave

& bends to gently touch & smooth
the cloth that wraps his corpse.

Sunday Morning

keys jangling, the janitor
begins his building check:
bum in the dumpster's
tossing trash right & left—

"open this fuckin' building—
they's cans in there, I got
to git them cans, I need
the money now, goddammit!"

a brief, futile argument:
the janitor backs off, swearing
he'll call the cops, churchgoers
in Sunday best parade by

arm in arm & view the scene,
turn up their noses in disgust,
to which the bum retorts,
"fuck you, too, you assholes,

fuck you"—who once was
a babe in someone's arms, &
cried for love, cried for
love, cried for love.

Pointing It Up

the whole city
spread below, he perches
on his scaffold

pressing mortar
into cracks, turning
his trowel with care:

eyes so intent
on his work, he's unaware
the wind is rippling

thru his shirt.

AP Wire Story: "Janitors at Risk"

For years I breathed spray paint, toluol, methanol,
xylene & hi-lo fumes under roaring fans
in the factory,
then coal dust in aging boiler rooms, pulled
        hot clinkers & breathed the fumes,
                inhaled
diatomaceous earth, muriatic acid & chlorine
vapors 6 years at Lincoln Pool, breathed
asbestos in boiler rooms,
in tunnels & mechanical rooms across the city,
        inhaled chlordane, wood dust, germicide
fumes, stone cleaners,
boric acid dust, ammonia vapors—almost my whole
        adult life—exposed myself daily to
                shit, piss,
vomit, mucus, hair, congealed sweat, menstrual
blood, as every janitor does. Today,
        meetings to save the planet
fill auditoria as janitors wheel chemicals for the
        air conditioning right past
                the door where
the speakers have worked themselves into a
righteous frenzy! O sacred soil, I knew you
                when as a child
I sang in your treetops & dove from cliffs to meet
        the river god face to face: I toss a handful
                over my shoulder

    & plant these seeds to keep this dream safe.

The Abandoned

A field spread
with dandelions,
stars thru which

boys race madly
in the cool spring
breeze—dusty dog

beyond the fence,
wagging among
rusted mowers,

old tires, a beat-up
yellow '57 Chevy—
hood up—& old

wrinkled mama
on the porch
sprawling on

a faded chaise,
watching her boys
go, they turning

to wave once,
shouts echoing
among tenements

beyond.

Pacific Sundown

across from Sheraton & ShangriLa
& New Belle Vue Bistro where ties & skirts
in shades promenade & raise glasses
to contract, deal, & faithful love,
homeless old & young slump on benches—
rusted carts, pans & clothes, backpacks,
bags, an old blanket shook free of dust
laid beneath oleanders & palms in the deep
Pacific evening. children with old women's eyes
stare at every passing shade. old man,
face & hands a web of lines, sings to himself
& claps, & claps. waves race onshore
yet none swim now: millions foul
their own bright blue waters where
native & european once looked out
to marvel in the fading day.

Sierra Madre & North to Oregon

imagine, she said, the mountains beyond—
white smog's too thick for us to see—
appearing at last, great wrinkled heat-browned

hills stir us; where now does the path begin?
-—endless silver streams of flashing cars pass
below, harried commuter frenzy—you unborn

generations curled in liquid dream, I hear
your diapered squalls & aging sighs even now
here where my feet walk & yours will walk—

what cooler sunrise will greet you, what
dewbeaded roses, windflashing wheatfields,
what delicate blossoms hang above mossbanks

& rocky beds of fishleaping streams? what
canopy cresting firs & pines new grown where
now stumpfields echo hissing winds & pyres glow?

Audubon in Fog: The Descent

thick fog on the peak above—
       gnarled whiteblack granite.

here,
 endless fields:
           yellow,
yellow
 delicate
     buttercups:

underground streams
 rush thru rock beneath.

above
only the cairns're now visible
in the white
 veil—

      my companions
somewhere above
 scramble down
as I sit here
 now—

follow
the cairns when the path disappears

 sit
until your heart

 beat
 slows:

                    if you
pick
 your
                way
                care-
fully thru this fog
you may
stay on the path.

                         still
the stones
            may shift under
your feet,
clatter down unseen canyons
 where you too
could fall—

catch your breath.

A March Blessing

sunsparkled floodwaters, glassy calm:
thousands of saplings bent at floodline
straighten to run at the sky! fallen

trees are draped with flotsam, leaves
& sticks & styrofoam cups, papers
& wrappers blown from the highway.

the old mounds are islands now:
ancient spirits sing in this land
above their bones & flooded skulls—

first buds swell, great ravens
stare from high branches, the wind
is just warm & fresh enough to turn

a busy traveler's head & fill
his dream with lazy song, hear that
falling water now; so I dream of you,

long gone! recall you racing naked
paths & count you still as one with me
here silently as I bring my son

to this shore for the first time,
to see the wild flights of birds &
know the tracks & signs in sand,

hear that open, quiet melody, breathe
that breath of river's blessing,
that calm & rising, falling flow.

Catching Nothing

thru the tentflap, with Anne,
      half-asleep, distant rumbling
            thunder coming on fast—

last night
I wandered in circles staring up—
      stars thru dark branches,
owls calling
valley to valley—

I dreamed of you, waking after
      102 years of dreaming
           enclosed in flesh,
      gone the dark way now—
visions of quaker
      ancestors passed, Wiltshire
           to Delaware machinists,
the dinosaur bone collector,
efficient & ambitious,
      whose skull is now some
      professor's paperweight—
& my grandpa, wandering
purposefully
thru his fruit trees—

the thunder's closer now, now
torrents of water crash thru
      dark branches;
the rain's steady, flood heavy—
rivers spring up in pathways to camp—
thunder *hammers*
the earth, which
trembles, shakes beneath us!
lightning arcs

143

thru camp past the tent, again!

we speak in high voices to be heard—

what branches above us might shatter,
crashing thru our skulls to earth?

we lean to the open flap to know
the splendor of the torrent.
in dreams my father
sails out of a starry night
past rocks & wrecks where
bones are washed & sink in sand—
            along Marquette's
last route to Illinois, who
            died bringing words
to natives who knew
            well enough the spirits
that speak for earth & water.

my father ages at the wheel—
hands grow gnarled, winds cut
great lines in his face, yet
his eyes flash as he closes
            on the dawn,
his genoa full of wind as he
            plunges thru heavy seas—
later, becalmed, he sings
            an incantation for the
beckoning dead
that he might move calmly toward their rest.

the morning after
is calm, cloudy—
fishermen wade in the swollen river,
            casting & casting &

catching nothing.

      the silent heron is still.
 deer
move out across the open plain toward
the lake, where they lower their heads
     & lap the still water,
ears alert in this intense silence—

       even
our hearts beat like
hammers now, sending out waves of sound
    over & over—
the breath
is a wind that
stirs up all the world.

For Helen Cope

the silence of an early Sunday morning:
jade & night-blooming cereus at the window,
flocks descending from winter fruit trees
to the feeders—my grandfather, autocrat,
could speak volumes in a tone; yet
grandma's quick eyes defined the silences.
waking children found an exact art in china,
silver, crystal & serving plates heaped high.
holding hands for grandpa's catalog of gratitude,
I opened my eyes to her smile. alone later,
she rode camels in Morocco, climbed to
Machu Picchu with an oxygen tank, undaunted
by thin air, eager to know the abandoned city
all cities bear within. she insisted on
dignity in age, grace in the human touch,
that we be honest with death, clear & calm.

Midsummer Night

thru vast yellow wheatfields & green corn stretching
      beyond treelines at the horizon,
nuclear power lines hum in forcefields from
tower to tower—farmers herd cows
to the troughs as I pass, lost among distant
friends in crisis. the evening
breeze is soft, the light rich & yellow.
      home, my children race among spruce
& pine, fairies in a midsummer night's dream,
      blessings in a sea of sadness. here,
someone's put a door on the old grange house,
      raised a frame for a room to be
attached, boarded windows that last week were
      open to the careless winds.
rotted boards are piled by the road, where
two girls are walking hand in hand,
arms swinging, their smiles only for each other.
      half moon above—already passions turn
like seasons—love, hold your shaky course.

The Abandoned City

if we sit long enough, will our love grow wise?
the roman mottos tumble from facades & crash.
where statesmen argued the language of law,
cedars split paving stones & broken pillars crumble.
atop the giant boulder, a maple's single thick root
grips granite all the way to soil below, where
we stand amazed. lovers go to sing their love
hand in hand, passing a drunken cursing hulk
who pitches headlong toward a red-faced hooker—
she shrieks, pushing trash cans in his path,
her mouth a red circle of moaning terror.
O air pregnant with mouths opening like new petals,
O silence humming with coos & shrieks,
O rays revving cells in a single juniper needle!

Convent Garden

where nuns once walked the cruciform path,
rosaries clinking in silence among herbs & new blooms,
now mulberry, box elders, trees of heaven spring,
mallow & goldenrod tower among ragweeds & wild
grasses gone to seed: the evening air echoes
old prayers, old songs raised in choir somewhere.
the wooden cross is weathered; where the body of
Christ hung, still-dark wood outlines his form.
within the convent, the drum thunder of
a native celebration announces a newer,
older covenant: a frail old woman,
her silver-black hair bound back with shells,
softly sings an Anishinaabek migwetch among a rising
generation—a hand stops the still-resonating drum.

For Fin & George

scarlet sundown tonight—
clouds of seeds rise & float
across fields thru dogwoods

& downy oak leaves unfurling
in this cool silence—
O Fin & George how share

your grief at young Fin's
passing, who gave sixty
dying boys & men

a brief season of hope,
who healed them with her
persistent touch & dreams?

today, my own daughter
sat & marveled over
the choreography of bees

in sage & columbine
as I held your letter nearby,
shook with sadness & dreamed

the tenderness of each dream
passing, each small common
loving touch. across lakes

& rolling miles, I'd sit
with you, to know your sorrow
& give what comfort I may

below these now appearing
endlessly spinning stars.

Farewell

skull & shell in rock where
the delicate tracery of nerves once
shot the gap thru living meat,
bone digit that once pointed out
stars or tenderly touched clitoris &
birth canal in moments where
their eyes drank each other in
& their skin was singing flame—

O song! rise out of that
dead mouth now! bright babe!
leap thru those jaws
into white air again! spinning seasons,
oceans, rivers, rocks & tides &
still dawn where one leaf floated
by the boy's dangling feet, who rose &
looked back once & walked away—

tonight a brother's greatest gift
to brother is letting the goddess star
guide that dark sail beyond
any horizon for the knowing: that gift
is tears, yet here's the heart
where kindness is more than kind &
kin is bond for breaking. farewell!
keep watch from that other shore,
we're coming.

The River

the heron bends; the silver fish leaps.
in seconds, the water is still again.

the woman in the funeral home does not speak
her grief: her eyes are wet. never alone,

we are always so. our two hands touch;
two rivers flow almost into each other.

full moon rising thru thin clouds
at sundown stops us—in spite of being

a common sight. white phlox, lilies,
coneflowers are still. processions

come & go thru church doors—
baptisms, weddings, funerals pass

year by year. tack when the wind blows
that way; say it & share it—tho

nothing may be said or shared.
in the blue evening, clouds of insects

churn above the still water. sitting
here, full moon floats below & above.

White Light

for Allen

              white light—
early February
      frozen winds
          despite snowmelt &
      patches of green—
flocks cling
      in kinnickinnic,
         wheel up into
the clear sky.
      how many days
& years have we
      left as friends
         moving among
the same silences?
      foolish to ask, yet
            how moved
      I am, just to
see you again.

slender Muse,
      trumpet this
         love among poets
           in years to come.

In Heavy Clouds, In Cold Rain

in heavy clouds, in cold rain
she bends & sings her daily pleas,
plunging hands into her purse—

she's lost her tickets, she
spent her cash, that dime, where's
that dime—loudly addressing *you*—

but she shouldn't, shouldn't beg
from strangers, how could she take
their *gold*—she's poor, we're

poor, we're all poor—how
could she—get away, devil, get
away!—shouldn't put your

hands on strangers—rolls her
eyes skyward where the cold
mist falls on barely frozen

January soil, on evergreen & naked
branches alike, millions of jeweled
drops pendant, as another

pilgrim paces nearby, turning &
gazing at her everyday chatter,
dreaming how a life could be-

come so tangled, what love deferred
or gentle heart denied or genes
awry to chant this lay, what

time, O bus be on time—you'll
be late, you can't be late, be late
in heavy clouds, in cold rain.

March

       as seedlings bend
whichever way the harsh March
light floods into the room, past
       flowering paperwhites
& Christmas cactus whose pendant
fiery blooms have long since
       dropped, I sit in the quiet
of the late afternoon watching
a grueling rush hour parade beyond
       as starlings in bare branches
leap & claw among swelling buds,
a frenzy & pecking order
       mysterious to the sole
singer in the silent dawn. My
life's more than half gone—
       the young singers who bang
on my door at midnight raving
with dreams await a tempest,
       will bend as I have bent
toward moon & sun that pull
whole worlds in lovers's eyes
       where dreams strut in flesh—
dust motes flash, green worlds—
& nothing sings its silent roar.

For All Lost Love

one needs to be
apart to find her
heart's strength,

trembles with new
silences, hearing pain
in her son's dream,

dreams how her
husband's love, tho
pure, could not

suffice. another
comes home to find
his wife has

broken all bonds
of love. he sighs,
lost in what love

might be, should be,
O sing for all lost love,
for love's dream &

sighs, for whispered
cries & tears, for
opening eyes.

"What Thou Lovest Well"

shape-shifter, master your veils
in the moon-spun night, dreamer
with the lyre whose tune spins

thru empty air to find the promise
in goldenrod & queen anne's lace:
the wind shakes the drying stalks

& voices echo in darkness spinning
light where graves release lovers,
who bend again in the turning dream

to veiled histories & manic songs,
drugged & dying in an endless dance:
what you love well will remain.

Each Wound Became a Voodoo Mouth

breathing fire. the acquitted officer grinned—
hands that crippled a defenseless King
waved in departing. gunblasts & fire followed.
she could see the flames from her office window,
carried a pistol in her glove compartment.
Koreans opened their shop to looters,
praying it wouldn't burn. King pled for calm.
white kids on 90210 partied on in the angst
of wealth: who'd get whom in the all-white
swimming pool? faces dripped blood,
scalps laid bare: fire—fire—
from the hold of the sinking slaver,
escaping slaves still dragging chains
broke free, no common language but anger—
their bonfires rose on the alien shore.

El Mozote

Abrams & Bosworth could not remember
those days when they took over
in Human Rights, at State. Amaya, hiding
in a tree, watched the soldiers kill
her children & put them to the torch.
in one house, the floor was blood-soaked,
most of the dead, children. "this . . .
could have led to the unravelling
of the US effort to promise a rapid
expansion of Salvador's military forces."
in La Joya, Lopez came home by night
to find his wife & 6 kids shot to death.
perhaps a thousand dead: Reagan certified
El Salvador's "concerted efforts" for
human rights. refugees returned
to the abandoned town years later
to say Mass for the long-neglected dead.

Poem Beginning with a Line by Pound

State of the Union, 1992

the enormous tragedy of the dream
cries out in the bent shoulders
of the peasant women of Moscow,
in the rough hands passing over
the brows of wrinkled toothless men
waiting in breadless lines.
Hitachi closes its California plants:
Mexicans will build wide-screen TVs
for a dollar a day. laid-off workers
may wait in unemployment lines where
the eyes & hands of mothers turn
to skinny children at their feet.
"those who aim at the rich usually
hit the poor": this *wisdom* comes
thru a boardroom smirk to a rising
rhythm of stuffed shirt applause.

For the Old Man's Tears

gentle night may share
her silent starscape's
dark & pinpoint fire

if we walk naked into
dawn where shining
beads shake out from

the phantom tree's
spreading branch.
the gateless gate is

swinging; the old man
may lift his eyes & know
his own tears at last.

Ghost Dance for *La Grande Vitesse*

in the deep silent hour
        my footsteps echo across
the darkened plaza—

the last homeless crone
        has flopped beneath
freeway pillars to sleep

& coke-stuffed yuppies
        roar out of the bars
surrendering to dreams at last—

only the wind remains
        blowing around the Calder—
rose of many red lips

moving together, bright
        dream in the old maker's
heart, aery steel

balanced & bent
        to a corolla of red
lips & petals flowing

in a turning dream,
        every curve a rapture,
a crying out—

Live, & swing with it,
        brother, sister. not much
singing in these

steel & glass boxes nearby,
       where the great cultural
statement is a bank note:

does the city know what
       it has? Do
the people hear that silent

singing flowering among them?
       it is not
in crowds come to gorge

on fast ethnic finger food,
       nor in
towering barbecue smoke

nor in the poetry, which
       festival organizers want
to be "suitable," "light," etc.—

nor in the yellow ribbon
       draped there during
the war, garish symbol

of our gorging on
       Iraqi flesh, our
mass-murdering pride—

but in the dark night when
       native shades stir
in the wind about

this rose, these lips—
       & the song mourns
rapids that once were,

Owashtanong once pure,
           & time when light
came in silence,

when men & women
           dreamed among the
million scattered stars

now lost in bombarding
           fluorescent flash
& smoke of *progress*—

sing, windy muse,
           of the dream we've
sold & lost, & live here

again among us
           shades to be
scrambling for

we know not what.

A Prophecy

the futurist foresees
another Renaissance:
forget the gold-maddened
strangers, children
baptized & butchered,
galleons & armadas,

dead natives displayed
in the London of lame beggars,
slave ships out of Africa,
a wilderness hacked flat
for forts & frigates
frightened pilgrims

become savage
buckskin invaders—
Progress! Technology!
better yet! we'll have
art & literature
borne of leisure—

dreams of eden do
persist tho the garden
be dismissed;
in the turning gyre
the Muse will now be
bought & hired.

The Lovers Sleep

all winter, the wind carries loam aloft from the stripped land;
the lovers sink further into sleep, the moon rises over
frozen furrows, & lines of light race across the vast prairie
where no man sings alone by his dying fire among constellations.
when stars fall, the caged shaman sings, his guards hearing only
silence. the millennium approaches in a raging human flood,
the swarming intellect polluting its own skull, cradle of dreams
where fields might blossom to meadows in singing silence.
the unruly master bangs away in the chest, summoning
blood & obedient hands to turn the wheel on which a sparrow
hangs & sings; tomorrow the shriveled finger points within.
so the lovers sleep, locked together beyond their spinning songs
in a dream where light rises to light continually.

Satie & Dante

in the silences between syllables, the path
behind us disappears; memories become other lives.
when the poet ascends into paradise, his carnal love
spirals into an ocean of light. what brought us
here? rock formations atop the volcano fade into
advancing columns of mist; a mad saint clings
to his perch on the path ahead, laughing, howling,
rolling wild eyes as we pass. he too grins in bones,
which rattle as he wails. we reach a point where
we no longer know where we've been, if love has
changed us: the day grows dark with light—
if we bring back stories of she who transformed us,
who will take the song for truth? such tones
evoke a presence dreamed & sown in tomorrow's soil
to emerge as new blooms for another's eyes.

A Charm

let worlds wake & petaled dreams
        unfold as they may,
infinite globes wheel regardless—

ant, spider, lion, man & woman
        turn in sleep
& stammering, sigh & wake as

the sun winks out passing eons;
        each passing
moment's jeweled lights blast

thru dawn's aspens, reddening
maples, oaks,
as ravens bend to scattering winds

& mock their yawp over roofs of
        this world, where
bones make data of fleeting dreams.

Silences for Love 1993-1998

The Rhododendron

for Suzy—"let's be famous lovers"

sunlight thru an open door,
crimson blooms swelling to burst:
who can say
what love is? you take a friend
in hand & roar down blind road after blind road
wandering thru private rooms
in each other's hearts, sailing thru whole histories
of pain & rage to find a quiet morning,
dew on the laurel leaves. love is not
in the eyes, in the heart, in the entryways
& hotspots of flesh, in heavy breathing—love cannot be
contained in soft arias
whispered at dawn—it is neither two together
nor apart: the eye
is in the hand, the heart in the eye,
the song exhaled & inhaled
& suddenly your dreams fill rooms where others
pace & sing softly of what you were—
O love,
steady rain on the city of the dead,
teardrop on a granite peak, clear day,
angel ghosts circling
the flowering black oak in every long-gone summer
night full of thunder,
sunlight thru an open door,
crimson blooms swelling to burst.

Alba: The Sailors

moon gone down, 3 a.m. starscape where loveboys wandered
hand in hand now obscured in luminous
grey light & the silence of pre-dawn breezes swelling
the curtains as one boy sleeps & his lover leans above, watching
the sailors hoisting bag after bag into the bright light of the cabins,
adjusting line & tackle, slapping
each other, prancing on docks as the horizon brightens,
still no sun yet already the dawn waves fill far out with sails
headed out & away, no destination but dreams in
fogbanks far north or in island romances spun by singers
in late night reverie. leaning to the window, he looks down
at his stirring companion, dark eyes & lips opening to caresses
in first light, & yet he is at once far away, looking backward
at the receding shore, bright day already rising to meet
         dawn's first rolling breakers.

Two Women Dream Together

staring straight at you, the first seated on a red chaise playing
soft guitar blues, turning to sing into her
young companion's ear, she leaning languorously,
biting into a nectarine as the boy brings them their drinks.
beyond, an old man dances quietly, hanging his head,
his wrinkled teats flapping in time to the balls of his feet
as they bounce & slide across the bare floor. Thru
the window, the rich yellow light of sundown shines
with dust, & far away one can hear hollow cries,
summons to prayer echoing away centuries & kingdoms.
the script for the song remains unwritten as the woman
throws herself into her play, her young & old companions now
frenzied, dancing nakedly together. here the cacti blooms
flash up like evening's white fire & by dawn
hummingbirds will suck the hanging fuchsia's nectar.

for allen

that summer in the mansion on the hill:
you & Peter in spacious kitchen
       fretting over chicken soup, seaweed, Tibetan tea,
the nightly readings—Chris Ide & I dashing thru
halls & rooms upstairs in our underwear, chasing each other
 giggling rowdies rolling across beds,
wandering in basement perusing huge library,
singing old Kerouacky Catullus Kit Smart
& Shakespeare's sonnets aloud together—
you upstairs all night answering mail yakking long
distance scribbling surprised by visitors
as I lay in the next room & watched the million stars
       fill the night over the flatirons, singing myself to sleep—

or that time in your apartment twelfth street I come
 to read in your Brooklyn series—
racing to work to class to plane Laguardia taxi-dash
downtown in bright springtime exhausted—Steve showing
 videos you at wailing wall & old Reznikoff
       our shared love introduced by George Oppen,
 steely-voiced compassion my reentry
into New York—gefilte fish, Peter & the Wolf
after everybody cleared out, you & I soft reunion,
 both drained in crazed worklives, both sleeping
20 hours waking together Saturday evening going out
 bite to eat at Christine's: NY Times, cabbage soup,
chocolate cake—a Danish family recognized you,
sent their kid over for autograph, you yakking
 & drawing elaborate skull & stars & flowers personal
greeting with final pen flourish for their bright eyes—
friendly, welcoming the parents their first time in America—

or that summer where you'd injured thigh, lay naked
 on floor your apartment Boulder as
young girl massaged pain spots, relaxed nerves
 & we sprawled around you,
            singing Campion & Dowland,
Steve as director who
gave us parts bass baritone tenor singing
            again & again crooning to find
            the shared voices in the dream—
 poets coming & going, staying a time,
always singing, singing deep into the Elizabethan night
            as Boulder's sirens shrieked
                    & traffic flashed beyond—

& in later years, both too busy, yet your call sped me to
            buddhist retreat Yankee Springs
 only 20 minutes from my home—
two afternoons scribbling notes together in lodge
 as Gelek spun the word thru Gun Lake sunset—
or meeting backstage after *Howl* & *Kaddish* Ann Arbor,
too tired to speak, no need to yakk, comfortable merely
 to sit an hour in each other's silent presence as
            stage hands gathered props & instruments—
your kiss disappearing into the night your hand waving
            pulling away—

& now, calling each of us before the press releases go out
 generous gesture even dying
passing burden & light from Walt thru Williams you & Jack
 thru those who remain
            to new nippled generations
struggling even now to be born.

sirens & flashing lights stop

        traffic where the strikers tried
to stop trucks plowing thru
their human wall
        & cops waded into
the jobless lines
collaring shouting men & women,
        tossing them into the wagons
& slamming the doors:
                high noon
        in the shadowless summer,
unseen eyes
peering thru the mirrored windows
                where others, jobless
for years or scrambling
as burger clerks, errand boys,
        part-timers & sweepers
to pay the rising
        rent & fill the hungry mouths,
succumb to
the scab siren's song of money.

The Cranes

silence, no stars in this black night: the sleeper's own face
stares back at him, empty-eyed, pale & blue, thru flashlit water.
ravens wheel toward the highway where black uniforms
sweep red-stained glass across the concrete in the headlights
of tow-trucks. angry drivers howl & thump dashboards,
hissing to be on their way. high on the mountain, a woman
carries a flame thru razored granite, near the dark summit.
radio clank of boots, boots, boots—a gallery: mouths of
the century's great politicians, their bright teeth, red gums,
tongues spitting syllables—for grasping fame, a hundred
thousand torsos split, skulls crushed, the famous last words
hissed to a brother as fire arcs down from above. clatter of
ribs played like vibes—flames sear even the highest tree—
cranes fly in line, leaving the lake, scudding west thru dawn.

Two Hearted River

eyes like ravens over road kill
        fingers flashing in reeling zebcos
                the fishermen can't grasp
that some come for
        the water itself, tannin-red
near shore but so clearly a black mirror
where no face appears—

        or for lichen-rotted balsam firs
lying like corpses across the flow stacked
        with flotsam & foam, feathers
& bones, the fallen gathered
        to spin in currents siphoned
& spat down where the portagers put in
        with a quiet rush
as cranes hang almost still in the turning
        sky above—yet

                even the heart
        cannot fathom what stillness
rests in this plunge, why men
        sing together like choirboys &
stop the gunnel rush &
        lay the paddles down in the
whipping breeze where scarred pines bend
        thru storm & sigh & rainbow's end—

        nor is it clear what draws one to
the mouth even as the last ice flows frozen
        in winter's roaring surge break free
in great chunks, leaving
        the churned sand of November's waves
again among agates below—

even the dramas of rescue at sea,

the poignancy of a captain's last
transmission, retold around
a kitchen stove in Paradise or Mackinac
       by old salts now retired
to muse thru waning years
with stormy Mondays & the names of the dead
     cannot pierce thru this water
        to the lost bottom
or read the runes in the lights of the waves.

He took a long pull on the stout, thanked us all, & disappeared into the night

after the governor
drove out the disabled, closed down the hospital
—oh, they're still here, leerin' out their grandma's windows
        or wanderin' in the street talkin' to shadows—
family's here, y'ain't gonna send 'em
all the way to Lansing & y'ain't got dough

        yeah, they voted in a new prison,
hungry for work—fightin' over hash-slingin' jobs in Marquette—
they strung wire, remodeled rooms, took inmates
        & now they parade around
in their new uniforms, with their pistols & their jeeps,
        but now they're payin' for it,
lights on all night—hell, y'can see 'em
even out here on a clear night—
& right in the middle of town, those lines
        & lines of barbwire bundles
        goin' up—preacher said they look pretty
in Sunday morning sunshine with the new rain hangin' off 'em
& then I knew *he* was nuts, too.
        That damn governor, though,
don't get me on him—that son of a bitch!

In the Alley

race your day
away, son,

the old man
spat, sucking

on the butt
he bummed,

& you'll wake
to find yourself

alone. he
raised his eyes—

the kid replied,
yah, old man,

like you know
anything,

pissing your life
away with *talk*.

The Job

years later, he'd disgorge monthly:
searching swamps & paddies for the dead,
       eyes in treetops for snipers,
he'd reach thru muck & gassy water
in tropical heat:
skin slid from arms like sausage casings,
arms & legs pulled loose from bloated bellies—
swollen eyes were open, white with decay.

       (get the dogtags &
drop the stinking meat into a body bag—
try to forget anxious parents,
the high school sweetheart now in college,
her perfumed letters,
his radio flyer buckskin fantasies, hip shake Watusi
& all those dreams of panting love—
       tally 'em up).

       he couldn't explain
to his girlfriends how even in their
most intimate moments that death smell
would come to him—he'd
       run shrieking into the light,
shaking, his tongue a babble
of dead men's names.
       even here, among
the laughter of friends, he'd need
you—to hold his shaking hands,
again & again, trapped in that dream.

Thru Gary & Calumet to the Monet

yellow acrid smoke once horizon-wide is less
obvious now, tho ruined ponds & neighborhoods
freighted with heavy metals still seem as bleak,
wedged between the wrecks of mills, refineries
in ruin, giant pipes & pulleys & valves rusted shut,
boarded warehouses. above ore-red shallows
& lime-green depths, the mill worker's rowboat
bobs, his line flung out for catfish who cruise
the slag-ridden bottoms for any sign of life:
jobless since Reagan, the old man lifts
his tattered straw hat to smooth his silver hair,
raising his eyes to muse at the endless parade:
skyway roar & magnificent mile, the delicate
lilies of Monet, the weeping blue guitarist who,
tho shoeless now on Columbus Avenue, echoes
in the *appreciation* of bankers & brokers &
republican art dealers, the intellectual elite.

push off

                                                  into silence,
steady
    snow falling, floating about us,
        high banks above, white swirl in

firs' rising ranks, gnarled cedars, aspen thickets,
    the high deciduous crown
in its cloud of white.

our paddles hiss & plunge,
    hiss & plunge thru gaps
        in the now-blinding storm—

ahead, wreathed in mist rising over
    roiling current, thru drifting snow,
        you turn to a hairpin bend &

disappear in a soft blizzard beyond:
    upright, stroking slowly, evenly,
        calm beyond command.

in the dark at last, we lie flat
high on the plateau, now clear night: crescent
        moon, ancient tales spun in stars,

Mars glaring on the horizon,
    still pools reflecting clouds & lights back
        into the sky as our breath rises

& disappears. & still later,
    waking in deep night's wild dream,
I look up to northern lights flashing,

                              flashing
ancient signals, flaring thru
    vast sky:

    you & I
small & tender in our moments together

as in moments others will share
    in time to come, relieved & awakened
        as we were.

Memory in Love

for Chris Ide

Venus winks on the blue horizon this evening:
my mad boy star-crossed rimbaudian dreamer
has passed thru the veil beyond agony with his

leaping poesy of fireworks for no tomorrow.
no simple song unravels the riddle of heart & eyes
tonight: go find your way, sing the pity of it;

hear your lover's sleeping song & keep that
tuneful breath as a torch in memory's night:
he was your friend & however fitfully carried

your dream in his time, juggling hope & fear
in the gleam of fading youth, unable to sit
long enough to give his own suffering space:

you who know love, go sing it now, hold
nothing back, let your sighs swell as paeans
to the long trip's passing under empty stars.

Many Reunions

old friends come
thru my door nightly,

long yakking,
cool night breeze:

their laughter's
what I waited for,

their bright eyes
& playful touch in

late night lamplight,
their valved voices

humming under
Flatirons' stars.

New Life

if I move beyond blue peaks
snowbound in July's high heat as
ranges float in haze like dreams

or fly into Newark thru storms
blasting wings to make strangers
gaze with dead men's eyes,

if I wander in the late night
with crowds of singing poets
among darkened homes where

whole lives pass, never known
to you or me, and if I scribble
love letters under street lamps

into my palms, or howl among
old boys as the round moon rises
thru autumn oaks, I keep you

with me always, always at my side,
your hand in mine always, serene,
leaping thru our bones to new life.

A Vision in Manistique

in vision the cities glare
       & groan beyond this horizon,
              in legend & shipwreck &

sweet home blues, the poet's
       graveyard of sighs, the young man's
              cry for industry & eloquence.

recall the dream: stars slide
       above the liner making its way
              from port to port, a faery queen—

the boy at the prow entranced,
       city lights now appearing &
              bejewelling the darkened shore

as mates stoke boilers to Captain's whistles
       & cardmen & brokers fill the salons with
              figures & profits, sophisticated chatter—

tonight, all is starry round, ancient shore,
       naked love in a young man's dream.
              the years dissemble; the song remains:

silence itself comes in waves to shore
       & summit & aery sky, punctuated only
              by the foghorn's muted timeless roar.

The Mirror of Heaven

tonight's beacon flashes above breakers shattering
spume over gnarled limbs & broken rocks as lovers

leap ashore like sailors gasping beyond the churning
surf of Seul Choix, hand in hand, hearts raging

for new life. crones & croakers stumble & sigh
from rock to rock, as surely alone as together:

inland, the blue-green waters of Kitch-iti-kipi reflect
"the mirror of heaven" where the ojibwe lover

drowned for Beauty's eyes & tangled hair.
an iridescent dragonfly settles on the surface, is

plucked in the instant of a trout's rising rainbowed leap;
shadows below mimic the roiling rings of waves:

shot thru with shafts of light, gold-lined
clouds race westward into gathering night—

a harvest full moon flashes thru this gloom,
splintering below to lights on breakers' rising roar:

we too have sung the language of tangled tongues
in the mirror of ruined dreams, & blindly sing on,

still in the silence beyond hypnotic roar & crash,
seul choix for sailors doomed to wake perpetually.

leaving classes

full of nubile women
& young men whose

eyes're flames, I drive
across town, dreaming

of my own children, their
aimless play, dreaming

of Sue, the years we've
spent in & out of love—

bright October afternoon,
maples tinged yellow—

thankful now the surgeon
found no cancer

in the lesion on my lip—
recalling years

I smoked & fumed & swore
there was no tomorrow,

pouring what came
to hand down my throat

for kicks, burning
for that lost high—

the hidden meadow

the long breathless climb
    thru meadows asplash in
        yellows blues & flaming reds

    around granite boulders
shattered upthrust shanks
    thru aspen fir & ponderosa pine

        as shafts of sun flash across
    a spring trickling down among
grasses swaying in early breeze—

    the city below now awake, faraway
        roar, metallic shine of grinding
    traffic bullethead race to deadend

routines in offices banks & restaurant
    chatter—but here the lovers
        wake & stretch together

    & wander from tent to sunlight
rubbing eyes scratching butts
as I pass unseen, upward

    to the hidden meadow's
twisted pine aslant the "saddle"
where in solitude's miles of

    jagged peaks cliffs empty trails
        the sun rises still & silence
    rings in these ears at last:

in this furious flowering,
  three ravens land & strut
    & eye me now, immaculate

  company in calm ache
of mind & heart, the raging planet
  wheeling where even love roars

in the void & every step's
  a ghost dance thru flames
to find the stream & float away.

  O moon thru the white peaks
    now! the clouds flash away,
  the land below lies in its

white silence where
  lovers turn to each other,
    the meadow now a dream.

all night

she lay thrashing—
cramped thighs,

her head in
waves of pain—

he had only
his hands, pressed

against her soft
flesh, caressing

forehead, eyelids,
behind her ears

massaging neck
& back & thighs—

little more than
brief diversion, yet

her soft whisper
drew him nearer—

no healing but
calm against

the worst of
her pain

For Martin King

who sang the flesh made word that bones may walk,
that none be turned away—we open the secret histories,
bring our varied carols together in dreams & signs,
each to each in turning gyre, on quiet stairs, alone on
the lost bridges of our desire where in vision we see
lights in procession leaving this shore by day & night
& dream the time to come: our word's our bond:
no pistol, nightstick, bomb or threat, no pallid law nor
crooked courts may unmake brothers & sisters. the bells
never stop ringing, echoing over Birmingham, Selma,
Washington, Memphis, ringing in Brooklyn & Los Angeles,
ringing where babes' eyes are rinsed in elders' blood,
ringing where ancient hatreds boil yet across the globe,
ringing thru the busy silence of every day, ringing in you
& me, sister & brother, ringing in our dreaming bones.

Turning

how long,
>   how long
>   you've been gone:
>   wandering last night
who'd I hear in the
>   whipping grass &
>   the ringing wind?
what'd I see
when the full moon
>   slid behind that fat
>   cloud? I must be
>   talking to myself—
who's walking
>   beside me on this
>   beaten path? No
>   one, no
one—a shadow.
>   a toothless old man
>   one-eyed, with a patch,
>   appears from behind
dumpsters piled high:
>   "wanderin' again, eh,
>   sonny boy?" turning—
>   only the wind, scraps
flashing down the alley.

no time to feel

my own death, flashing past in roaring freight train blizzard winds,
to see lovers friends my kids' eyes fast forward life scenes passing—

all these cars ahead in ditch & overturn pile-ups cop lights spinning
up & down the lanes, new arrivals fishtailing slamming brakes—

& suddenly I'm in it, hit the brakes, slide sideways 50 mph past
two cars out of control, their drivers' eyes wide, terrified—

I pass in unreal slow motion, turning, turning, hills & fields &
faroff lake, farmhouse & barn half-glimpsed thru raging snow—

spin the wheel & somehow come to dead stop, facing south:
a woman stands knee-deep in snow, quaking hands wiping her eyes,

her car overturned in the ditch, cops racing toward her. rear view:
others're bearing down on me, they too sliding out of control—

time to move—hands shaking, tapedeck shine a light blues elegy
filling my survivors' ears—get up to speed & breathe that sigh at last.

April

battered in the frozen storm,
                    ragged
          seedless
tufts atop
browned stems of last year's
pampas grass
          scrape & whistle
in bright sun. April 1.

          the rivulet
becomes a flood,
then subsides.
          those not swept
away sink roots
further into muck
& grow.

what stirs at the base of these
          singing stalks?
who can
swallow the sun, speak in flames,
 turn the world
green? that voice raises
 continents,
shatters mountains,
changes tides with a word—

yet almost silently
a single drop beads & balances on
          one unfurling leaf now
open in the hidden meadow.

Free Clothes

a young woman, somber in her worn dress,
dark eyes staring at the faces in the hall,
runs her hands thru a small boy's hair:

he fumbles at her side, arms about her thigh,
shyly glancing into the eyes of the big man
who brings the clothes. within the dimly lit room,

an old man, hands contorted with arthritis,
fights his crutches, cigarette in his shaking hand,
slumping at last into the couch between

two fat aged women, who talk softly, thick arms
encircling his bent shoulders. the morning's
warm: they've made it thru another winter.

Turn the Wheel 1998-2003

Lost Loves

old man slim boy
& boy-to-be, I wake in the cold
moon where even
the crickets lie silent & the leaves

    hang in the flooding mist,
black streets silent—
even the midnight
screamers gone to bed at last—

& hear you though lost forever
singing in my ear, feel your
tender touch as you
    stroke my forehead—

so many gone down
    the lost river, so many waiting
now for you & me to
join them, singing

in some night apart,
    shadow faces alight with
secret fires, love that floods

even this room if only we
    turn to it, & make it ours.

Fran

I see my parents still
        wailing in the living room Argentina Street,
a grey day, no wind
& out the window traffic flashing past—Aunt Fran's
        husband & son Dutch, my older cousin who'd
filled his room with electronics, a genius at 13, killed,
accident in the Rockies,
& she in a hospital, her arm broken—my first
        memory of lives, faces swept away from my life—
later, when the sun broke thru,
wondering where we go—I was six—

& after that, Dutch's oak furniture arrived,
        his bed to be my bed, his mirror where my face
would stare back, sigh & dream of love—
& Fran, recovered, circled the world alone, sent me
coins from England, Austria, Egypt, Japan,
        mysterious envelopes that arrived in the mail
worlds beyond my suburban sidewalks
& mystery gardens where I'd pause
        before an open rose & lose a day in dreams—
        later, her house burned & she escaped
        miraculously, settled & worked in Maryland
as my parents' marriage cracked up,
grandpa died, I raged at fallen love & lost my heart
        until, lost child, I found myself in Sue
& found my father again & heard
        my long-lost grandma's sighs,
                Fran the oldest child who'd seen more
& kept herself apart, learned to be alone—

yet after the loss & the fire & the years apart,
        she met her Hale & danced in her 70s like
                a teenager, a few years without pain—

a few years blooming in the fullness of her womanhood—
        who guesses how much we can know even of those
nearest us, how others cope & sing above their suffering?

she'd refuse a funeral, would
        go home to lie with her Hale—
        these last months
awaiting an end that now comes swiftly—& I, learning of it,
        sit with my sisters & my family, my 50th birthday
stilled in this quiet moment filled with her life,
flocks of birds wheeling in slow motion, hovering around
        the feeder in winter snow—

Solihull to Marylebone

fast train past a fox & her kits in bright morning sun,
           a child's basketball stuck
       between tracks at Leamington Spa station—
      row houses fenced in & crumbling—
what eyes peer thru these begrimed windows, survey
their lives in these cramped yards?

onward, to London: scotch brooms & queen anne's lace
          doilies to the tablelands along the way,
 farm wife waving from her backyard to kids
running thru Albion's long fields, legs stretching beneath
         faroff hills & gigantic clouds,
hundreds of sheep & lambs gamboling beyond—

now singing gangs of football fans,
Manchester United red & Newcastle stripes pile aboard,
 charged up for their collision at Wembley today—
        how many sorties over Kosovo today?
I dream back thru an evening in Coventry, Alan's talk
      of firestorm during the blitz

& the revenge bombings in Dresden, always
        the little people *getting it*—
roasted alive, broiled in their shelters—
Churchill's on Millennium Contest signs
in the supermarkets where Englishmen wheel carts
in silent pleasure picking out their next week's fare—

what shall I see when I finally come to London?
     Julius Caesar, enacted again 400 years after
Thomas Platter saw it, with concluding all-male dance—
    the blood of centuries spilled again
for the blind seer's sighs & the blinking wise.

Reading the Signs

                    far from the main track
            we push on
                    thru old loggers' trails
            crossing & turning upon themselves,
across the stream
            below the roar of distant falls,
into the dark,
leaping from boulder to
                    boulder, over
            the shoals onto
the morraine's high bank, clutching
roots & gasping, crawling upward,
                    no sign of the watchers
            tho their eyes were on us—
thru the abandoned
            ruins, crumbling brickwork
still standing—
deep in the valley, harvest moon
            over the last hill behind us,
crickets
            crickets trapped in the last
desperate
song of their lives, & still no sign
            of the promised path—
crashing thru twilight & heavy brush
to look up at last & see
            the moon beyond the hill
& now the faint trace
            of a trail, where we see
at last into each other's eyes.

Ghazal of The High Plateau

mesmerized on the trip to this high plateau—the barren
promontories, windswept spruce giving way to high scrub

& thence to rock outcrops where marmosets chattered
your names to the wind as you sang, half in your sleep,

tales of desert sun, wild waves on faraway November seas—
recalling the fallen hiker, his bandaged legs straddling his

giant companion, weary eyes haggard in stubbled cheeks
whose lips whispered only blues—time passed so quickly

you hardly realized you'd arrived, & now, with news of
loved ones dead beyond your grasp & hopes, you turn

to vanished loves, vanished paths, & find no way, even
the path behind you vanished in clouds & mist, only

glimpses of far peaks & guessed-at valleys ahead, even
the cairns indistinguishable in rock scree. here, there is

only one tiny yellow flower, an unearthly flower, nameless,
a crooked flower once signed to you by a long-dead sage.

this is the sign you were to wait for: consider your frail
bones, aging in the meat of your boyhood leaping,

those aches in loins that once propelled loves & led to
singing heights, that song which brought you here, that

you might sit. the mists are the myth of this season;
 the next path can't be seen with living eyes; the heart's blind

cupid can't fathom the love to come; sit. even the light
will spill in strange showers over your tired limbs & into

your eyes which, blind until now, will open to the shadows of
meadows & peaks still unknown. in the dream, deer

paths now blazoning broadway, towers stacked high with
grumbling dreams & cell-phoned illusions melt away, as

does the day you were stopped *still* before prairie-wild
grass, the sun blazing lights & shadows thru waves rolling

to the horizon. old friends return like wild leaves in moonlit
valleys, sit & sing in your ear. the mountain is not

the mountain. inside the vanished waves, beyond
mists & lost paths, songs become pathless riddles in

your white hair & aging eyes, your child-corpse moving on with
naked winged feet, the unearthly flower now a sprig

at your ear, as you sing silence at last, a breath, an ayre floating
beyond this air as surely as you yourself were sung.

Tender Petals for Calm Crossing

along this silent path among cliffs thru terraced green
you'll sing beneath your breath where the poet dreamed

his escape thru the clouds, where whole populations fled
to rebuild shattered dreams, hands in the moist earth—

stone masons who shaped the rock attentively, that it
interlock & honor earth that gave both seed & harvest

in the sweep of seasons—ghosts today, they wander here,
picking your pockets, to know what dreams you bring

to this place, what breath you leave among these rocks,
what song you gather in your backpack & basket of silence:

here, a lost mother weeping for her child borne to minutes
of love before its last breath, the father pouring a lifetime's

devotion thru his hands, his face red with defeated love yet
shining in all the brilliance of that loss—here, the lovers

moving together, their short gasps echoing in a great sigh
thru which another child comes—here, the lost father who

could not face the wreck of his love in his own child's eyes,
his sorrow a hermit lost in the passes of his own valleys,

heart bursting with roses he could not bring to his own table—
here, warriors cut down like corn on a day as crisp

as this, eyes turning skyward one last time, up to the light
as their blood gushes out on fertile ground, shining path

where arms & legs of the dead clutch & kick at heaven,
vanishing dreams of hungry ghosts. so you come, bringing

blessings & eyes to flush the tears that still pool in the world's
grief thru all the rages of lost centuries, all the weeping sisters

crying for lovers who never appeared, all the lost brothers
marched thru barbed wire to death's final anonymity

in the last bursts they'd ever hear, minds turned inward
to their mother's cries on the day they forced their way

into this light, compassion now for them all: that your dream
be clear when you come to this pass, I send you this wish

where tender petals turn, open in both darkness and light.

The dharma at last

longdead in his dream the boys leap
        one by one over the cliff into the wild splash
                & the singing current—the tow pulling them

        down into green dark & silt where the sunken
trees fell & were pinned as well, great black
        branches looming up in the murk, fish tearing

            the guts of whitened & bloated corpses as
        their eyes stared, marbled spheres like moons
glowing in the dark. by night, the water clears, the

shadow moon reflects off the pale carcasses—
            & he is awake, panting, the moon shining
        thru his midnight window. he hears the voices of

thousands singing & weeping as police line up & swat
        batons swat batons swat batons & march march
            march into the now-screaming singers,

        their ranks breaking—the one-eyed bard chanting
for calm—the ranks all fled, he left alone to sweat on
        a factory floor, in a madhouse swabbing urinals.

            now the dreams are moonlit, no destination
        & yet this weary traveler sings in his passing
steps, careless in the theatre of stars where the dead

        walk with him daily, nightly, old companions
            urging him to rest as even days grow darker,
        the news ever more ominous. he must consider

the sleek craft of his final voyages, the turns in his
        last river, the song he will compose to take him
                beyond his last lay to sing in dreams where

        his companions fled, to learn to walk among
the living like a shadow in the daylight of
        their certainties, waiting for them to leap at last.

ER Saturday Night

           she staggered out of mass after delivering
scripture readings, burning
pains in her chest, face flushed—

now, he sat by her in the ER, silent years
           flashing by in a confusion of images, wedding
                      bells & tenement years & groping thru babes,

                      miscarriages & shitty jobs, her eyes
           now questioning, she talking thru
                    her pain as the interns wander thru with

questions & routines, the machines above—
           green readouts, peaks & valleys charting breath,
                    pulse, life itself—clock relentless as an admitting

nurse's keyboard, the drunk two sheets over
           howling at the attendants, "fuckin' bastards, you
can't do that to me, try it, you fuckers, try it"—

finally, she must stay the night—blood work,
           chemical readouts, studies to see whether it was
                    indeed a heart attack—& he is out, in the cold

                    night among the stars, helpless, looking back
           at windows where she might be looking down, her heart,
                    their lives, in the balance of relentless day & night.

In Silence

for Ann Barber

hour after hour
they waited in the ER,
expecting the onrush

of wounded & maimed—
yet there were only
firefighters with

smoke inhalation,
cuts & bruises, hour after
hour, the minutes

ticking away, the dust not
even settled, filling
the winter garden, the palm

court, where no
wounded walked nor
rescuers bore the maimed,

only the silence &
the realization at last
that none would come

thru the open door,
beyond the shrieks & sighs
& the endless roar.

Blue Notes for New York

a winter of dust & paper
fills mouths & eyes—
faces forever racing away,
in terror—

even in the rising sun,
the bright day
over battery, harbor,
Liberty herself,
ships speeding away
toward Jersey shore—

so many gone down
the dark way for nothing,
amid flame bursts
& bodies falling
thru spreading smoke—

in dreams, millions tramp
thru centuries down
Broadway's ancient
native path,
golden door with its
open promise,

rush hour crowds,
saxophoned canyons'
bleak light: here a blue note
for your long night of wails,
a paean for your
fallen dancers' hearts.

Ground Zero

high in the tower
rush hour headlights stoplights
metal traffic

below, office workers
streaming thru doors in a hundred buildings—

two sit on the stairs holding hands,
one stroking the other's hair—she
in tears looks up as

a dark stranger's shadow passes down
into the stairwell below—

she waits until he is gone,
turns & folds her head
into her sister's arms.

Bomb Fragments, Body Parts,

where Taliban fighters once
camped & awaited their day
of glory, their welcome from

seventy virgins in their
imagin'd paradise, the piles
of rubble're all that's left,

two men picking thru
looking for unspent bullets—
blue sky above, line of brown

ridges valleys snowy peaks
beyond, telescoped goat paths
where generations once must've

hiked in silence & heard their
hearts, singing to bell'd herbs,
dreaming under a blue moon.

now, far above, jet trails
mark the horizon where others
drop bombs or die for

the same oily glory, blasting
away for their big holy chunk
of the gasping planet.

The Disappearing Sages

as Voltaire would disappear thru poppy & hellebore,
        thru primrose & the endless sighs filtering from
                half-opened windows of tenements & prairie palaces,

        out the door forever into the meadows of waves surging
toward the vast rocky plain where barks & liners lie
        broken, their treasures of bone & pearl & shattered steel lining

            the stream like broken teeth, so these last voyageurs
        push off & disappear in the opaque mists each dawn,
leaving the world to scowl & threaten, as it will. So

        missiles careen into Palestine as sunflowers of blood,
            the hotshot pilot shaves a spyplane's wing & ejects
        into the wide wide sea, into a woman's tears & memory;

the pimple-pocked grads paste mortarboards to their heads
        & march away from their billeted dead aching
            with scars in their eyes. the magus himself must

        break his staff at last & pass even his third thought
as vain; courtier & statesman machiavel it to the end, where
        the last standing man is Caliban: thus the journey out,

            the relief & laughter beyond the perilous voyage,
        the farewell to the alchemy of the word, the silence
that illuminates & heals the brainsick heart at last.

The Gift

where nurses scuttled years & machines clicked & whirred,
pushing air to lungs that they not collapse about his heart,

the room now is silent: no more parties with eyelids taped open,
no Indy 500s surrounded by old friends who in later years could

only squeeze his hand or massage swollen feet until circulation
returned, briefly, the soles grown warm—no glances back to

the boulevard of broken dreams, his days as a James Dean
in waiting. nor will rockers blare Clash songs from the roof,

bring roaring sirens up the drive on the 4th of July—no more
mannequins'll be blown up with dynamite, nor will wild boys

ride off lost trails drunk with visions. The ordeal of years
put the clocks on hold tho lovers & family held up, somehow.

now he's only for the faint stars, finally out from this last
station, this prelude to silence. today brings the gift—

that he was *here* so long, that he endured, silent, & kept us
strangely clear thru his silence, now at last set free.

Gone (as you are)

when the currents push you
       straight into that hairpin turn where
           slammed sideways around
       the bend two fallen mammoth tree trunks, stripped
           & bleached, lie along each bank,
branches forcing rushing water into
           a narrow channel—brake
       & cut thru surging waves, avoid the crash
              that'd toss you into the roar the
frigid waters, your craft swamped or adrift in
       wild plunging currents—
somehow you're through,
          the river widens out,
     calm, & you can
sit back as morning sun fills forest & swamp.
          ahead, deer wake to your imagin'd silence,
leap for their lives
       through cedar budding kinnickinnic giant firs,
breezes raising whitecaps racing
       toward you, & you await the moment when
the wave line hits & you lift your eyes
       to the new sky where
all the sleepers are finally pushing seaward skyward
       in a mad rush
where the cranes lift themselves & are gone,
       as you are.

Owashtanong Sunrise

light breaks in the racing waves,
            hissing currents roaring around
                  pylons, across shoals—
hidden rocks
                  send up plumes & roostertails
& swirling flower-eyes of spray—

(here a thought of you who'll stand where I now
                  stand, & you who waded along
        this stream & sang for fish,
pronged stick pointed for striking,
                  & you, who watched aghast as logjams
        upstream cascaded in *debacle*, crashing
thru bridge after
                  bridge—lumber barons uptown splitting
        dividends grown from their grasping hands)—

        now one greybeard bends,
                mutters & sighs aloud in the stream,
limpsy jaw & chicken-flesh neck
working the air with syllables,
        machine-like,
as he plies the currents,
                casting again & again, no luck—
    no luck—
eyes turned up to you in brief greeting—

then a strike, & both you & his chatter are forgotten—
        his bandy arms now wholly turned

to his task, playing the fish back &

forth thru currents—
                    wild rolling silver streak
            flashing in the green spray—
the old man's legs braced against a rock cutting the stream,
                    the fish now cresting the waves,
leaping & plunging beneath again,
                    then gone . . . .

            he pulls the slack line in,
                    opens his bait bag
fishing around for a big one, turning the hook to take
            a wildly wriggling worm—
& casts again & again,
            flowers of spray & lights like eyes
                    still flashing about him.

the white-bristled sallow face in the photo

has clear blue eyes & no family. the preacher who'd
begged him each week—"come to the mission where we
can help you"—brought him a flannel shirt & chicken soup
& found only the rumpled sleeping bag, scraps, the cold
corpse strangled & heaved among pylon stones—for what?
under this overpass, the traffic roar of thousands soars
thru this hour of pearl sky & red-lined clouds;
the lights of downtown offices already wink & shine,
reflected in the waves below—in the Amway Hotel,
hotshot conventioneers & stock splitters fork their eggs
& lift their glasses, pause & muse at the passing water:
a swan has landed in the eddies not far from the leafless
red kinnickinnic & poplars whose buds already swell
with spring, near the graffiti'd wall & landing where
the old blind trumpeter blows each morning's blues like
a funeral hymn, welcoming hikers with his bright eyes.

After Ronsard

among wars rumors of wars faithless
century faithless age angry politicians—
among a thousand trials, ancient freedoms stripped away,
surely it's madness to speak of Love—

chained madmen, fanatic terrorists're
no less mad than I—I,
grizzled and sickly, who've grown eyeless
as Love itself, insane—

imagining lovers falling for each other
among fallen towers, dreaming of love
among threats flashing across airwaves—

adieu, weird sisters, spellweavers, politicians—
Muses, I shoulder my own sack—I'd rather
pass trials than go blind on your aery streams.

The Fourth

       She came off the plane from
Macedonia in tears, unable to speak except with
hands & eyes
       the anguish of two lost sisters,
 their children, their families,
how would she find them *here?*

       her husband worried
their luggage wouldn't make it,
       talking, talking, his hands wringing—
the last remnants of a life forever lost.

       within a week
 he'd have a garden in, turned with a simple spade,
his cabbages & peppers & shallots
growing in this new American soil—

yet she alone,
 dreams shattered
beyond internet Red Cross listings & English lessons,
       would stay at home,
inconsolable—

In a Sentimental Mood

like Trane's mourning sax wailing deep night streetlight sorrow
he waits & watches her disappear beyond the illumined circle—

out his life forever gone to another dream—he, stood up among
backlit waterfalls in wheeling traffic, before a statue "the gilded hero"

like headless Herakles stoptime gliding toward hopeless distant
towers lit up forty stories of shadows groping in fluorescent lights—

the night shift, heads bent over desks hunkered down like deadheads
groping for tomorrow, for bleak sunshine factory smoke steam vents

rising thru naked trees stretching like spikes skyward, vapor trails
beyond, endless graveyards tombstones angel wings weatherbeaten

granite tears, ships beyond freighting grain fords computers to green
breasts of land, wild ports' hubbub swarming sailors longshoremen

drunken deckhands, ears fulla other news—ships too at docks
disgorging blinking immigrants eyes glazed dreams of starry nights

wading en masse to stare up at blinding lights traffic roar fumesighs,
old worlds fading in memories clutching at a word an icon a shade—

he wrapped now in her retreating steps—those nights they once held
each other for life, shared warmth final defense against the loneliness,

the roar, the nights of sighing down their separate screams, all gone, all
gone down, song for a lost embrace, a kiss against the sighs of dawn.

Canyon Rim to Hopi Point Sunrise

the fabled domes & vermilion spires, towers, ledges, pinnacles
shine faintly in the distance, pale blue, ghostly by moonlight,

frigid wind slashing up the canyon—one picks one's way
thru scrub pine twisted into spiraled grey struggling out of

the unyielding mesa thru centuries of weather, passing bands
of hunters, warriors, tourists—here where Cardenas stood agape,

where Anasazi & Havasupai measured their days in tales spun
in fire, I grope thru the dark to sit alone, silent under the fading

blue horizon, you lost to me as a bright dream once floating
in a still sky—yet it is good to lie flat to fierce gusts,

on a stone ledge jutting into this deep emptiness, awaiting
the first sun shafts white light flashing up thru the canyon,

& then to turn like a bright angel & make my way down
onto pack trails, switchbacks where as the sun mounts higher

ravens circle above, their flapping wings like sails slapping
in the breeze: thus one may greet a new day, beyond despair.

Lear by Lanternlight

        white moon now
    thru the tent where
Poor Tom brings
    his old father up to th' extreme verge—

my companions asleep
    far across the clearing, their
        logsawing complement to roaring
            winds above the highest firs—

this a.m., their kayaks were
    taken in raging cross-currents, yet one
dipped & feathered merely
    with a paddle tip, & found the center—

to float where the heart
    slows, the ear tuned to
        the humming of that silence
            none hears in the smug city

    where blindness comes not from
cruelty, but the stealth of routine—
    even such an eye-
        less man may need to see

        his life's a miracle, O moon
thru my tentflap now—

Yeah, an' here he was,

leaning down on me with his one eye still
full of tears, the other now gone blind,
singing an old yiddish ballad in my ear

like some long-gone yenta come back to
find me a boyfriend—I'd been dreaming in this
mile-wide field of headstones, the glassed pillars

in haze beyond, & distant rush hour thunder,
wealthy slaves still quoting stocks & haggling
in their hopped-up SUVs whistling while they

race to work—& above them, the raging torrent
of dead souls screaming upward like roman candles
into the mild sky toward the emptiness beyond

pole star & lost sailor alike. singers of my generation
disappeared like evening rain when he left, burrowed
into silent meditation in moonlit mountain cabins,

working on dreams deferred, hands rough now
building invisible stone towers & tearing them down,
learning the meaning of silence. a new breed

now runs the show, drives the planet ever closer
to mammon's nightmare circus, buying, buying
to save themselves from themselves, never

looking back, racing like mad horses for some
lost nowhere horizon. once we'd thought to howl
them back, yet there they go, ears ringing with

cash registers & cellphones. the heart's no longer
heavy with the grief of loss; there are light moments
when one may sing with long-dead friends,

watch dreams walk lightly from the living tomb.

"La Goulue" Considers His Lines

O, I could wow 'em
when I had the stage—
I had those boys
singing in the aisles
calling out my name with *roses*—
      O those hip shakes, O let go!
      & wild, wild eyes every night
under the lights—

so when you called, I o'erlooked
      my torso, once without a stitch
(oho!)
      of fat, & saw I'd not be what I was yet
O the hap of it, to be
in my chartreuse gown & my
      feathers again, to sing &
            leap again—if only once—&
feel my legs carry me up
      in my fishnet stockings & slippers, to
turn again & sing again—

so I dream, alone on my bed, & peer
into that mirror & see
                  that sweet-faced boy now
      valiantly—is it age? hoping
to live out some fantasy?—
      or art, the love, the *feel* of it—

moving out into those lights &
      just letting go, letting be, the rush of
breathing in a wild turn,
sighing, again

              & again, beyond the *image*
          we make for ourselves.
O to come again for you,
come once more
              to that dazzling light!

Madadayo in Dreams

deep moonlight, blue night Norway spruce ginkgo & apple branches
        shadows across fresh snow blue-white,
even roaring trucks up on 28th muted in this stillness—am I awake?
        Sue asleep by my side, sighing, turning, & now

I'm floating, up into stars in murky dark where old Allen still grins
        & weeps in dreams, his basso profundo echoing beneath
3 a.m. ayres & madrigals springtime pretty ringtime friends giggling
        thru parts chorus of madmen warbling in the dark—

& Chris, long dead now, heroin overdose hot summer night, blue-faced
        corpse once genius riverboy who couldn't run his demons down,
parents' religious cramp desecrating his death, legal injunctions against
        publishing his gay poems—madboy Chris, coming back

to reassure me, "yes, it's as empty as I'd surmised"—young wino
        who'd strung himself out with me, raging thru poems late night
in garage, smoking pack after pack of Camels, spodiodi shouting darkly—
        they now vanish, their white eyes & bones melding into starshine,

singers gone back thru dream—how float thru these middle years
        so many shadows clinging behind, still keep that simple riverboy
dream intact? running crazed thru classes appointments meetings
        conferences medical pokings bank & billpaying—where'd the time

go how recover that stillness gone like my own half-forgotten child's cry
        when first I felt the pleasure racing naked in woods & diving
deep in sunken pools only to find fish eyes staring back in murk?

        Ah, Jimmy, you shoulda been there when we hung high in air
before plummeting down the long waterfall into the abyss & rose
        like angelboys flashing up thru turbulence to stretch for the sun—

out, out, awake now, out of this dream to find the first purple lines
       of dawn, scratch my bum & flip the switch to a new day coffee
& soft Satie before others stretch & fill my ears with songs—
       wake to a third thought not my death, not yet, madadayo.

Out thru the eye beyond the stars

upriver in full moonlight, past the forested bank
where the old hunters' lodge once rotted away, even
the bars on the windows fallen in, beyond
the flatland where I camped, a boy, & dreamed
of Anishinaabe & voyageurs in the deep night—
dreaming back to that night when, drunk, we plowed
upriver on a pontoon in deep fog, Charlie falling
overboard again & again, having to be fished out,
Todd & I like lookouts for stumps in the swirling
current. now we approach the darkened banks & turn,
& I think of you, far away in the firelands, grieving
with your mother as her lifemate begins his journey
beyond this void: I'd cup my hands & catch this moon
& send it to you the way sages once drank this light in
& sang their lovelong death songs as journeys out
thru the eye beyond the stars, opening in tears.

The Night Blooming Cereus 2003-2007

The Night Blooming Cereus

night blooming cereus
tender petals open
fully long enough for

the moon to top
the trees beyond,
swarm of stars above.

in this garden stillness
I remember you,
Robert Hayden,

your gentle eyes.

Masks of Six Decades

shining day boy, sullen gangster, mad child, naked dreamer—
I chronicled blue-collar rages, sorrows, quiet lives, meditated
in boiler rooms & dreamed I'd tamed the dark shapes within—

now I eye them, sleeping, turning, formless, always present:
I no longer trust my own sanity. my children have risen
to their dreams; I wake to my beating heart & sigh. wanderer,

I lose myself in sunlight bending thru a vertical shaft of cloud,
rise on what thermals remain to the mountain cave where silence
beckons & the singer folds his arms to rest. strutting corpse,

will I end singing my blindness, visions borne beyond lines close
to the nose, go out dancing in Blakean light or rage against
the night? my father, now quiet at family fest, eyes me,

sighing softly that he must cling to my arm climbing the stair,
patting my hand, curious still that wheel spins within wheel—
& my mother, ghost in a wheelchair trapped in memory loss mid-

sentence, listening uncomprehending as voices wash around her,
asleep in syllables chanted for her, sky changing thru her window—
what nightmares each of them let go down the meandering river

in the long turns of their days, what sighs & rages, ecstasies, lost
hopes to get to this quiet hour, grave dreams still held at bay?
the world will not be moved by words, tho poets would have it so:

we sing our lives out in darkness surrounded by friends if lucky,
as any good man or woman dreams & is no more. the fault is not
in words, & despair yields no vision upon which to hang bugle,

drums or lyre: I'd have many loves shaking hips to a wild beat,
solitude within dream, herons gliding upriver thru dawn mists
beyond these eyes & still-beating heart.

To the edge & back: the gift

for Melissa Wray

gifted with vision to stare into midnight's
tears the sighs of
thousands wandering blackened streets
dimly lit in careless laughter & rolling

eyes masking the desperate reach
for a tender touch too oft denied,
trapped in shared sense of tyrant time
passing into the bleak hour pearl hour

where the solo trumpet struggles for
minor key solitude, the mirror reflecting
that empty stare where
she too had drunk & seen the spider:
waking in a haze, surrounded by nurses,
doctors, endless questions & her own
confusion, wondering how to phrase it, where
to begin, how to give breath to words the ladder out:

today, she sits with me & I cut the apple she has brought;—
bright morning, the sun shines across the succulents
filling my room, shining over her neatly coiffed black hair,

across the desk where we lift the slices to our lips & talk.
now she must choose her path, now begin a journey anew
& I a midwife-sailor she has chosen bid her welcome to that

casting off, beginning in bright sunshine solid land receding,
bid her trust her little craft & sail it beyond that tragic shore
that she find the word the key the gift she has lived by.

New Home

Boulder Creek races to meet torrents racing down
to join the Colorado, farmer's ditch along front yard
diverting some waters to those farms out east,
running along edge of his new home. crescent moon
overhead splashes light over rock face & spruce-lined
valley barely glimpsed above. cool wind—no guests now,
only dreams: a child's footprint, a path not yet seen,
a parent letting go before passing, silence that belies
echoing young revelers in the street. he has ridden
his wild horse to the edge of dawn, sung healing songs
that opened an old man's eyes, yet found no succor
in the badlands or in 42nd Street rush hour crowds,
the madhouse rush up Broadway. on his porch,
the pale ghost dance rings his skull: hands intertwined,
 riddling song on silent wing.

Hostas

29 years at the print shop, exhausted,
obsessed with retirement—fishing on Lake Erie,
smelting up north in spring—
bosses fired him just short of his full pension
& he came home, fire in his eyes—

                                        now
he digs hostas from his garden & sells them
two bucks a pot lined up in his front yard,
saws lumber for birdhouses to pattern so
his wife might paint & sell them at craft sales.

                        he's done the rounds,
worked maintenance at the truck shop,
run stock at the greenhouse, nothing to keep him
straight with hellhound bill collectors,
two years till social security kicks in—

he wanders in his garden, kicking clods, waiting
gun in hand for a rabbit to go for his seedlings.
he cannot talk about it—
heart pounds so hard he worries—heart attack
like his dad.

wild clouds race over treetops on Memorial Day
& he dutifully raises his flag to fallen comrades,
their memory still fresh as the day they dropped
                        before his eyes.

Abu Ghraib

the prisoner wears a black pointed hood; he stands, arms
extended as in crucifixion, wires attached to his hands.

who set him up like this? what parents, sisters, brothers,
childhood friends, neighbors, knew who could snap this

memento from the cage? & here, a grinning man, arms crossed,
& a woman leaning forward laugh over prisoners jammed

together naked, heads in hoods. this man & this woman—
what hearts beat softly as they returned to their silent rooms,

alone? or this woman who smiles, thumbs up, fingers pointing
down at the cock of a hooded prisoner, hands tied above his head—

already she claims she was forced, others were responsible, yet
now the prisoner cannot live in his own home town, shamed.

here, the corpse has a bandage under his right eye, agony stamped
in his dead face: he is wrapped in cellophane, packaged in ice.

After Lope

languid lines, mad thoughts
ripped from my rabid heart,
children of scorched eyes, speared ears,
heaved here enraged, unfree—

abandoned, lost to the world,
so shattered & changed
you could only be known thru
the blood of your dreamsighs:

since you've stolen the bullboy's labyrinth,
the waxwing dreamer's high flights,
the sea's fury, the flames of the abyss,
if your serpentine dreams won't accept you,

leave the earth, dance in the winds
& rest in the eye of the storm.

Haditha

mother & child
        shot as they knelt
                in prayer—powder burns

where the slugs
        entered & tore flesh,
                blood erupting into dry air—

even as marines
        moved on to machine gun
                a man, his wife, his daughters,

the blind old man,
        father reading his Qur'an,
                the grandmother, mother,

brothers
        & uncles. one survived,
                playing dead beneath

the body of her
        brother, his blood
                covering, giving her life.

Desert Serenade

even in shadows of death by fire, one dreams lost
lazy July rivers, loves locked in memory's starry kiss,

the long-envisioned trip home, tearful parents—
time's illusions stripped bare now in the blinding sun,

the sudden crash beyond the vehicle in desert dawn
brings one back & here she sat—2 RPG duds thudding

20 feet behind—lock & load, & there, not 30 yards away,
one ran for life as another furiously loaded another round,

aiming at her as she aimed at him—so easy to take down
black silhouettes, unlike the living man beyond one's sight—

their eyes met, & then he turned and was gone—
she shouted down later for not pulling the trigger.

Marines with cobbled armor

fight thru blind streets, windows where
killers' eyes could be staring down even

now—the camera follows a lieutenant
who'd talked of struggles with morale,

bright face self-assured despite doubts—
now in combat charging with his fellows

then screams & fire, bullets thudding
above the wall where the camera catches

one shrieking he's hit, he's hit—call it in—
puddle of bright blood spreading

on the pavement below: here on TV
in the locker room where boys & men

leave the showers wrapped in towels.
eight stand again before the TV, still—

one has dropped his towel & stands
hand over brow, mouth open, naked.

October Surprise: An Absurd Reverie

Thanks to Ed Sanders

in october may banjos, guitars, & violins serenade the clouds,
open the heavens that the blasted & broken dead may rise
from mass graves & sing again in voices unscarred by war—

in october Pablo Neruda will return in his centennial year
& sing again the heroism of peasants, that they labor sans layoffs,
that they have sunflowers & sweetpeas before their windows

& songs rising from their lost bedrooms in the starry night
where the moon shines over the sea, that the lost dead
thrown from airplanes may return, that Pinochet may wake

in his own nightmare & sigh, that Allende may rise from the sea
& proclaim victory. may George Bush & Osama bin Ladin
kiss long & lustily, make up & dance a duo in tutus

by moonlight; may Saddam Hussein & Donald Rumsfeld
exchange their grinning skullfaces for the faces of angels
& may they learn the ways of angels; may they learn to sing—

may unknown genius rise in the land & discover energies
not tied to black gold pollution; may the cartels fade away
& the armies lose their weapons. may soldiers awake to find

themselves naked in the sand & recall the hours of sandplay
when they first discovered their nakedness & their hearts
beating to a tune not devised by the musicians of hate.

in october, let there be a surprise so absurd none dreams of it
in earnest: let lovers emerge from the corolla of sorrow & may
they proclaim a free song that heals planet & heart altogether.

Rush Hour in the Swamp, Near Hopewell Mounds

hard enough
              dark in savage rain lightning flashing
  lane to lane,
              no time to linger on men pulling
          up nets on
the river beyond,
              butts in mouth
                  —fish flopping mad dancers
              struggling with their deaths—

              no
              time over here on the highway beyond
              sleepers in the mounds—
SUVs ram it right up your rear, racing
              to their own deaths cellphones
                  in their ears—
BLOWOUT—
              cars skidding every way offroad

              rolling metal lights flashing ending
              on their sides,
others askew
              stopped dead above, stalled drivers
              shrugging it off as a
door pops open below
              & a face emerges in flashlights—
figures running in the dark—rain now
                  hammering roofs &
              road & swamp alike.

May

new graduates recite Stevens' "Earthy Anecdote" to parents
& friends, tossing umbrellas among their breathing lines as another
backs them, trumpeting "Ring of Fire"—all in this clear bright day—

snow drops, crocus thrust, yellow forsythia, girls wild dresses flying—
white dogwood stars emerge over purple allium swaying in soft breeze,
blackberry flowers, iris purple flags wrapped tightly—

"up and down, up and down" springtime pretty ringtime madrigals
waft across a meadow in sunlit day, the gardener bent to his work,
digging, planting, finches' bold yellow high in the river birch beyond,

& in shade, sage & sweet grass smolder in a cowrie shell: beyond,
the news is plant closings, suicides, workers over the edge no place
to turn, missiles & bomb tests, bombings, mass rapes in Congo—

another would visit his daughter, bulled his Harley on a two lane—
drunk pulled out in front, he slid, bumped up, tossed, head bashed in.
surgeons removed skull top to relieve the swelling, he in coma—

old friend who'd sung & danced with me thru early middle age, now
living on a prayer, friends & relatives turned inward on his breath—
here a dream time rose for him, poised in an old poet's silver hair.

Last of My Singing Fathers

In memoriam Carl Rakosi

passed
          dead (you might say,
           not one to mince *words*),
          the century gone to bed
with you
Carl, quietly
proud
to be Charles, Churl, free
          man beholden to none—
         standing
with laborers
on the street, no
poet sitting on his exquisite ass—

at eighty,
reciting your epic elegy on the decline
         & last days of your word brother
George Oppen,
you demanded only
         silence from your audience,
reciting lines into the darkness
        that we all breathe
together more deeply
into the unmeasured silence that
        the voice itself
find its own inner rhythm, dissolve—
a heartbeat—

        aged sailor afloat among endless
stars & winds, no regrets, bemused,
        surprised, aware—

you were amused, too,
when Allen Ginsberg gave us
oatmeal & seaweed breakfast
then took a call & castigated his caller
(who would've cut his balls off,
blaming his religion)—
                        bright morning across
the kitchen table, bowl of fruit, open door
& breeze among potentillas beyond—

so Carl I salute you
old friend who signed me *ally*
when we read together,
who later recommended the sephardic poets
                        of Spain & touched on
the Jewish Eagle in thought—
                        last of my singing fathers—
small wrists, fine eyes, gentle
                    touch, yet
                        firm & kind

A Midnight Rose for Michael Pingarron

news of your quick death left me dreaming that night
we shared hearts at poets' party in Hoboken, you struggling—

speech impediment, immense passion for Lorca's *verde que*
te quiero verde & the great Pablo with his ear in the sea,

we too groping with surreal dreams in the museum of meat
as small talk swirled around us, one-night connections links

to worlds with big dreams & sad sheaves obscure fame.
all that was long ago, ages passing in a flash your poems

arriving by mail, your phone calls always timed as though
you knew I was headed out the door, stopping me for poetry

gossip & political outrage—your struggle with those who
would've kept you from teaching kids in need because

your speech was not theirs & yet we poets both knew
those who kept you from your hopes would never know

the worlds freighted in a word as we found them, intimate,
singing. now you're gone, & I see Bertha alone in tears,

despite family & friends around her, & pray she'll find solace
& keep your shared dream like a lock of hair in an ivory

heartcase, & you, dear Michael, when you reach that final pass,
look back & see poets hailing you with raised hands, & turning

to step through, look to see Federico's green eyes & Pablo
whose ear fills the sea waiting to greet you in that clear dawn.

Big Sale Shop, Bargains Galore

rusty bicycle bent rims & seat 15 bucks leaned against
a wall among spindly dandelions, dead yew branches—
inside, rooms awash in mildewing *For Whom the Bell Tolls*
first edition, how-to-books, *Life* magazines—thirties stars

& ranting politicians stare out at long-vanished audiences—
ceramic vase three raccoons striped vests playing banjos,
Charles Chips can stuffed with broken eggbeaters, old
spoons, motheaten stadium blankets Go Blue, racks of vinyl

Bing Ella Frank & Elvis still crooning in long-lost dreams.
three graces lavender-silver hair alabaster skin poke thru
photos: boy soldiers heading off to war stiff with rifles,
girls posing in new dresses flanked by gaping first dates,

grandparents in Adirondack chairs beers at the beach,
little dog leaping up for a hotdog, dad's crooked smile—
broken wall clock above, Father Time on faded dial,
thin grey figure tux & top hat white beard thin-lipped grin—

among cracked frames discarded prints & paintings,
a battered set, Chinese summer mountains rise
above plains waves & rocky shore, peasants on ponies
making their way thru forest turning up switchbacks

toward a summit & sky only distantly guessed at: "well,
how much ya willing to pay, how much?" hawklike,
the old woman peers into the eyes of an aging man & wife,
searching their souls as they glance back to the mountains

& turn toward each other, she thrusting her raucous laugh
into their huddling talk. She raps her fingers & sighs.
"look, I got a season closeout—will ya take 'em for 30, eh?"

The City in Agony

July heat wave, crowds loose on the street,
first dates strolling pub to shop,
old friends meeting downtown after
hot sun on the beach—
lovers hand in hand, strolling in a warm evening—

    3 dead here, 4 dead there—
hysterical news anchors
& commentators piece stories together from
bystanders—
cream lincoln with spinners,
    a grandmother opening her door
to find daughters & granddaughters butchered—
wife, daughter, parents shot together—

    downtown bullets
shattering windshields,
high speed chase wrong way on the freeway &
flight overland to a home where he took hostages—
    bullet to the head in deep night,
the house surrounded & floodlit.
freed hostages in trauma,
police struggling with fatigue & horror—

now silent contemplation, now sighs at dawn,
the city stunned in its own silences,
the backward glance, quick
steps where the city laps the shore.

Seul Choix Shoreline, Owashtanong Dreams

that night after the storm shattered trees & roofs, a double rainbow
hung in the black cloud & fierce yellow sundown over the hills—

hordes filmed it, cellphone lights lifted high over their heads—
stilled within, I wandered through the wind-whipped city dreaming

spring daffodils in new grass, wind combing thru in waves,
a crowd outside the church door following the hearse, the bell

tolling, tolling, corpse sprung to its last fall—earth, tears, roses,
memories flooding the stifling air, love letters fluttering in the ears

of those left. turning, I dreamed seul choix stones washed across
in high waves & calm, two lovers picking their way along the shore

no moon, their destination unknown, yet loaded with hopeful packs,
bent backs awaiting the dawn where they would finally sleep.

beyond the dawn, I put my foot down along the Owashtanong,
I sit. this is no song of age nor youth, the ease of the decades—

wandering heart come to light at last—this is not the weariness
of the hard slog in the visionary night, only the stillness after

the long haul, the vigor of coming dawn, the ever-lingering shades,
lost loves reaching out as morning hands to wash your eyes anew.

Frail Dreams (2008)

Frail Dreams: a suite for my mother, 1923-2008

As my mother lay waiting for surgery

in hospital gown covered with heated blankets,
twilit morn gave way to dawn, rush hour traffic racing
beyond August's ragged leaves still in this pearl hour.
she looked as one already dead, laid out still,
chin tilted upward, brows & cheeks sculpted alabaster,
the babe asleep within—I dreamed of all those passing
the night awaiting day to come, imagined processional
in silent light, & wept in the profound beauty of death,
unseen companion always by my side, patient lover
who brings the skull's eyes into the babe's heart,
whose song is an endless float where does & fawns drink
& lift their eyes to recognize *you*, whose dewy footfalls
break the strong man & give him his tears, who fills
the silent woman's tongue with words: even now
my mother opens her eyes, wondering if I too am still
by her side, I dreaming of my own children, of the day
when they'll wait patiently by my side & know this song.

Starlight Call

brothers & sisters
call back & forth
frantic—

she's confused she's
got piles of dirty laundry
can't remember what she

said when said who said &
now she's lost a whole day—
uncertain what happened

between dawn
when she was following
doctor's orders

(going to breakfast)
& the starlight call
when, strangely alert, she

remembers she should
have gone to
breakfast & can't figure

what passed
between dawn &
dusk—

& now, the brain scan,
the terminal
waiting.

Fallen

scarecrow sitting up, bony fingers clutching wetted hospital gown,
rounded shoulders, trembling legs, she seems the death mask of
a former self, round moons of her eyelids alabaster like the eyes
of tomb statuary—she trembles, startled by my presence, eyes now

wide—alert. her mouth opens, she struggles to form syllables which fade
even as she mumbles in tongues, hisses, sighs: "what did you take from my
plate?"—there is no plate, only a teacup with teabag, perched above
chickenflesh legs. her eyes grow large, she now sees me, sees that I am

David, not Charlie, closes her eyes when she talks or looks away, hands
grasping the urine-stained gown. she will not look me in the eye.
little to say, though she is quick to ask for her walker—I think, so she
might rise to use the bathroom. she takes my hand & looks away, but can't

get up. the fall has made her weak, feeble, forgetful. the nurse comes
& stops her escape. she looks at me again, startled, closes her eyes quickly.
her breath now labors; the nurse reassures me it's only Cheyne-Stokes. I
watch her breathing & think of her evasions: so much pain between us, I

the eldest, "beloved," whom she once "would have smothered" while she
could, as she brought me from the hospital. how does one reach through a
veil, through a death mask, through the blind eyes of a lifetime & somehow
find the love that must have lived once? at last, leaving, alone, I drive to my

next station, dreaming how we usher out those we love whose love always
had conditions. I am the sorrow child again, lost in a wide sky where tears
can't show what the heart cannot fathom, where the heart must indeed be.

Death, you come

to speak to me thru your mask,
         you touch me thru my mother
                  who now is dying, & think

                  to make me shudder. I see
         her as a child with all those
dreams a child bears like fresh

flowers in baskets to an aged
         mother, all those songs dancing,
                  dancing in Memory's too-large

                  ears. I see the ingenue
         standing at the church door,
triumphant with new husband,

their faces full of light,
         & the agony of divorce,
                  the lost dream, the struggle

                  to provide for innocents
         floundering in painful streams,
the aging woman emerging

alone, gripping that rage
         like a wand, a chalice
                  with bitter dregs for all

who cross her. Death,
         tho you have long sung
parting songs in my ear, I

see now only an old woman's
            tears, & I a sorrow child
left to bury a broken

dream, to sit quietly
            by the grave of sorrows
& clean out the store-

house that others may
            dream anew & let go
as they too flounder

& find their way
            on the stream where desire
could break all to pieces.

Frail Dreams

half in the dark, my mother & I await the meeting
that'll turn her to her next dream, assisted living or

warehoused nursing. she is frail, lucid even in
illusions, singing French songs she'd played on piano,

now recalling voices already lost in her recent past,
her skin still alabaster fair, eyes bright, unsteady

even in her wheelchair as the nurse wheels her
to the conference. the therapist is gentle, yet as

mother hears at last that she will not return to her
former room, that she must turn to the next phase,

she looks down, her mouth open, then blankly up at
me, at Charlie tapping notes on his laptop: we

see the other side: the phantom doctor calling
at 3 a.m. with advice to take gingkoba, emails she

sends on a computer she gave away 6 months before.
therapists and nurses smile slightly; she cannot

walk nor dress herself, is sometimes lost in vague
time. would she like to see a private room in nursing?

The black bees

quick banter swells from mouth to mouth
& she cannot keep up—her eyes move

across her now-grown children's faces,
questioning. frail, she does not speak.

gaunt wrists rest near unfinished ice cream,
sunlight in chiaroscuro thru the window.

pleased that they're here, she cannot follow.
later, under the courtyard's rickety pergola,

she is solitary in her wheelchair, oblivious to
conversations continuing around her, her eyes

above—black bees move from vine to vine,
busily engaged, the white clouds passing

slowly beyond them. she follows the bees
with her eyes, her head tilting and turning

as they move. I, the eldest, see all, but
do not intrude. for today, this is enough.

Between Sleep & Wake

as I cut the cake & we sing, she sleeps, wakes, startled—
her long-dead sister Phyllis is depending on her, she has to

get it right—don't let the planet stop turning, it has to—don't
let it stop. . . she sinks back in sleep, head on her breast,

sighing. we talk, we eat cake & ice cream, & watch her. she
wakes for a bite of yogurt, two. sometimes she finishes

half a sentence—stares into the light, our faces, her hands.
Charlie spoons yogurt; we plan our visit with the nurse.

later, as she wakes, I lean to her ear & whisper: "thank-you
for giving me birth. It *has* been a good 60 years"—she

is briefly, fully awake, searching my eyes. will this be
her last smile, the last soft laughter we'll hear together?

Her New Room

no longer conscious, she lies propped up, head cocked back,
breathing heavily, mouth wide open. we sort her things—
what stays, what goes—load furniture & TV she'll no longer need

& run it to the van, not knowing how much time remains.
her chair stays with the fiction that she might muse in it,
look out new windows. we pin up photos of grandchildren,

bring favorite statuettes, a poster, knick-knacks for her wall.
we *would* disperse these things now before tears shake us, yet
would not leave her new room without signs of what she was.

when she wakes, briefly, she stares sans recognition. there are
no words except "water," choked out from congested lungs—
yet she cannot drink, descending swiftly to a fitful sleep.

Mais où sont les neiges d'antan?

what became of the girl whose dreams dressed up for
Madame Pomponelli's neighborhood fashion show,

the sixth grader who skipped on sidewalks to French lessons
with Miss Meloche? where the girl whose father sang

"if ya can say it's a bra brecht moonlicht nicht,
you're all richt, ya can," she whose mother slumped

to the floor with paralytic stroke yet somehow endured,
the girl chosen from her dorm to speak to reporters

after Pearl Harbor, summoning words to guess the pain
that lay ahead? where the bright-eyed wife & mother

confident in construction site as her children climbed
dirt hills nearby? where the mother finding marvels

in screech owls screaming in the dark night, the woman
sobbing thru the wall, she whose fiction hid why he

didn't come back, she pleading with a son who howled
& refused his father on monthly visit? where she who

worked beyond limits, drove thru snows men shrank from,
she who stood by children who had no other succor?

where those early years whose endurance was celebration,
before marriages, children, distance, tangled memory

would divide us in ways we couldn't foresee? where she,
now reduced to labored breaths & sighs, long sleep?

Last Look

the room is silent, empty but
        for the bier. she lies, sheet
draped over her body—

she is so *small* in death—

the head tilted back, eyelids,
aquiline nose, cupid's bow lips, skin
translucent, alabaster

yet still lovely—we are

in tears. my lips touch her
        forehead goodbye—cold,
heat & struggle all

gone in the waiting day.

A Dream of Jerusalem

for Jaume Plensa

if in time the city has been, will be desolate, scattered bones
chirping in dry day, the woman calls her lover to come away,
searches without finding, sings silently that none turn to Love
until it descends in morning dew and in calling doves.

as bone fragments & ashes swirl in shining waves, sink
into dark murk & are gone, one turns in dreams to the child's eye,
the dark circles of bone where the mother's vision once stirred—
where her cheek met the small hand reaching thru space:

we are creatures made of words rounded by incantation
& the great lyric dream, the fullness of young lovers sharing wine
in the moonlit night in the garden, swearing they'll not turn to Love
until it descends in morning dew and in calling doves.

here, in mountain air & silence before dawn, in the spirit
borne of blind sight, cross-legged, the shofar nearby untouched—
in this heart shaped by words there is a presence that could
in a soundless tomb shiver the dark with hammers, sound

the call in waves shimmering in all the wheels turning across
the universe & make seraphs weep. yet there is the stillness of
the word, the child's mind that turns to her mother & touches
her skin made of words: words that measure breath to be

shared as tender touch in passing time: brothers cry out
at prison doors, women sigh in their last dank beds, boys turned
men shoulder rifles behind dusty tanks & blood is the cry thru
a thousand cities. here there is silence, here light & form where

words bring the lovers together, here the dream of soft bodies
moving together, the vision at once the child's cry & the mother's
last gasp exhaled in fierce sunset as if none may turn to Love
until it descends in morning dew and in calling doves—

here the desolate city, deserted temple, the lost tribe: here
the dream wrapped in words that round the breath in silent air:
here the ashes that once were man, the bright sigh & endless night,
here sun disc's eternal round in silence, unheard music of spheres:

let the woman call thru the city & on the mountain for her lover,
and if she searches without finding, she may hear the scattered bones
chirping in the dry day & sing silently that none may turn to Love
until it descends in morning dew and in calling doves.

Crystal Lake to Beulah

the lake at sunrise, cloud
shadows play across far hills—
my friends asleep still—
silence on the waters. I hike
to Beulah for bagels & coffee—
last week, I kayaked at dawn
on my childhood river,

spreading rose petals across
the water three years after
we spread my mother's ashes
below the spot where she
sat alone, to collect herself
beyond the wash of sorrows,
job & family needs—here

to hear herself in treetop
winds, in owls calling
tree to tree in the dark—
how little I knew of her,
really, beyond the mixed
signals, blue-sky woman
who barely masked

the darkness within, even
as I struggled with my
rage & tears. the petals
floated on the waves,
the bright chatter of my
siblings echoed in slicing
paddles to the far shore.

now, as those I love sleep,
the lake is still, & I hear
my steps to town, pleased
in this brief reprieve.

Flight to Phoenix: A suite for my father, 1920-2008

The Swimmer

thinner than the robust
old man they'd remembered,
tentative, he gamely steps

into the pool—a purple splotch
along one leg where
he'd fallen down a switchback

& skidded along loose stones
to a painful stop. his shanks
quiver & he trembles, reaches

for the post & bends,
laboriously foot by
foot down the steps, surveys

the water for a free lane
(kids splashing, a middle-aged
man in dead man float), then

slips quietly into the waves
where he assumes
an elegant breaststroke

like those his children had
grown to expect these last
50 years, a form so one

with the water that others
applaud silently—turn & bank,
turn & return & bank again.

Flight to Phoenix

in seat staring out window at clouds,
I look into my empty hands—
think of his face, my own a mirror
thru which I can see him
& in his, the pattern of my being.

I followed his canoe, early evening, he
looking back as I swam my first long half-mile
as he later followed me up Bright Angel.
how much sorrow we both contained, how
many tears, madness we passed & left, to keep

the heart secure. he was a deliberate hiker thru
sage & castled butte, his camera imaging the mirror
of our days: a fly on yellow cactus flower, walls
of vishnu schist, the son's full stride on switchback below,
the thousand-year handprint in Sinagua doorway.

In My Father's House

we walk thru his rooms, sit where he sat, tell stories—
the wild ride back from Hana, his teenage self scaling
Long's Peak on the front face where none now climb,
hiking beneath Tahquamenon, vision thru falling water,
the eagles trailing the boat a mile from shore—
the silences are deep, hollow, empty. sometimes we slip
& speak of him in the present. out his windows browned peaks
rise against the clear sky. the saguaros are in bloom, acacia
throw out bright petals. the mirror casts backward thru ancestors
toiling land & turning lathes, scripture ever in their hands—

Quaker faces lit with simple gifts, always the shadow
in the corner of the eye, the evening dance turning, passing
time & light, beloved who bears one from the dark
wrapped in blankets beneath the still moon. I am rapt,
shaken, & he is with me, looking out thru my eyes,
his hand my hand in the garden, cutting, giving life.
yet he is not here, a breeze in the acacia, then silence.
how swaddle myself with blankets long vanished & recall
a father's eye overlooking my child-sleep?

The Empty Chair

now there is an empty chair when we gather, for him—he is
in waves lapping the shore at Saguaro Lake, in the breeze
at the Muskegon breakwater & on your brow as your craft turns
in the currents sailing surely toward Mackinac Turtle Island—

pathfinder, he is sure beside you when you survey pines & birches,
lose yourself in tough memory in Phantom Ranch Canyon sunset—
his hand takes yours when you push off into new streams, daunted;
he is still beside you, silent, sure as a full moon in empty sky.

desert sunrise, saguaros in bloom, sotol plumes & skyrocket phlox,
lush yellow-bloom'd oleanders along the path all bear his signature.
the empty chair shows we are all beside ourselves, & while the silent
night bears tears, memory is also a mirror wherein we find the seal

& imprint that shows we are his, that the shared sign in kin & kind
is our charge & journey we make, the absent presence borne within.

Tahquamenon

I felt him
            near me as I descended the stairs
alone
the falls we had shared roaring beyond—

distant thunder
crowds on the viewing deck
and below me,
tannin foam swirling cloud designs—

he was there
beside me, briefly—
then I was alone, the wind lifting the leaves

the laughter of my grown children
coming up behind me.

River Rouge

after Charles Sheeler

Faces in Shadow

toxic clouds roil & pass above—
specks land
                  in the unseen housewife's
fluttering washlines,
in the nostrils of the workers—

here, the machine itself, "functional
            architecture" half-distorted barns,
half featureless rectangles—
the river, reflecting this
ochre & brown geometry,
the treeless land—

yet *nowhere* in this landscape do we see
the armies of workers marching
thru the doors at dawn,
chatter & coffee & taking in
            the enveloping roar of the machines,
leviathan

eating them alive, the
mad labor of the assembly line, the men
sweating, pulling, turning,
teasing out parts and forms
            forcing out Ford's cars
robotic in
dizzying line, ears
gone deaf in the noise,

bosses above
counting down every movement,
measuring time,
measuring the men themselves to see what more
they could squeeze
        from blood & bone.

Beyond the shadow

My dad grew up in the D,
his dad a mechanical engineer
redesigning high speed

pipe turns at Con Ed,
his childhood neighborhood
        raising three to be trans-

national corporate officers—
        by day a wild flight of kids
jumping off roofs, racing

        thru back alleys—by night,
families cowering in basements
as Feds & the Purple Gang

shot it out a block away.
        he'd dream back dancing
whole groups of friends

swinging to the Duke & Goodman,
& there was the "Battle of the Overpass,"
where Ford's goons battered

Walter Reuther until his skull bled,
the workers "sticking to the union
                'til the day they'd die"—

& as a young married man
      he'd lock my mother in their
            apartment, braving

machine guns at intersections
to get to his job working on
      bell housings of Sherman tanks

         during the race riots of
  '43—Hitler still rampant,
first islands pacific after blood & fire.

The Scythe

My grandma died at Eloise Asylum
now a phantom ruin—still standing,

empty halls, paint peeling,
a fading stone in the cemetery.

I was born at Women's Hospital
& saw Ted Williams hit one into

the center field upper deck at
Briggs, Kaline hitless that day.

Later Janis Joplin played the Grande,
the Stones drove 'em crazy at Olympia—

Motown rose with muscle cars
on the Reuther, the riots of '67—then

burned out years & neighborhoods,
ruined homes & blocks, the Rouge itself

become a relic of another time—
ghost world of shades chewed up

in the scythe, Time itself become
a tale buried in the lost villages

of Anishinaabe & voyageurs
filled with the light of the forest,

who fell in love with this land of waters.
& I come back & dream my grandfather

toiling in his garden, my dad a boy
again, his dream of the D & those men

who sang these streets & turned
lathes & worked the lines, hopeful.

Happy Birthday: you'd be 99

When my father was 70, we hiked the Kaibab together,
spent the night at Phantom Ranch with snoring men,

woke to bunkhouse breakfast, marched up cliffs
switchbacks sky & shadow, returning to our loves.

71 now, recovering from hernia surgery, I recall his
quick health, mind sharp at my age. Still in dream,

I keep the blossoming saguaros, eagles trailing his
sails, my earlier years of silent rage, long walk thru

dune woods with tender leaves of sassafras and native
lady's slippers blooming, as we crested the last rise,

the great lake at our feet. we talked thru those years
and found ourselves again, together in landscapes

suddenly home: the shared rush of Tahquamenon,
my first long swim at age 9, he following in the canoe,

watching over me.

September Moon 2009-2013

Andrey Voznesensky

who could begin
as Goya
eyes ripped out bomb craters
        bodies hanging like cracked bells
in a burned landscape
voiceless in the stunned silence—

who could continue thru such
shattered architecture
        where even corpses dance
as vapor, in a cry
present yet silent
among a generation without grandfathers—

the burned ends
of fingers grip the pen in agony yet
echo a darkmotherscream
        begging you
to bring lilies of the valley to your
mother while time allows—

Andrey, calm voyage now
among the silent stars. your song
        cchocs still
in the sunlit evening where we
murmur
peace for those who remain.

Emile at the Crossroads

Too many hours too many nights in the mirror,
hiding, running, his eyes now bulging in daily nightmare—
the helmeted gunner, machine gun spraying near naked

bodies, wrapped in blood mists jugular spray
as they fall, corpses bulldozed into ditches eyes wide
in death, & he, standing along a ditch—he, spared to

finish the work—he, looking into the blue faces
open mouths disappearing beneath a wave of sand,
neighbors, lovers, one hand last to sink beneath—he—

now at a downtown intersection alone with his
clutch of daisies & one red rose wrapped in green,
the anniversary of Heloise's disappearance, she who

had sustained him, her red hair like a fire
in his brain, her impetuous smile & blue-eyed
laughter at his angst, a tender touch, a moment

shared where they could reach into silence & hear
the lost songs, now gone forty years, now a dream
he clings to, awaiting the signal to change & let him
         go, far from the maddened traffic at last

March

white dawnlight thru my windows, thru fronds of cycad & spathphylum—
fierce light after months of storm & sigh, turning from death to death—

now foreclosures—gruff men once hipsters or marines hair trimmed back
after thirty years, pushing mowers shooting hoops with kids, thin women

with long hair & hard wise eyes, tough women at the mailbox, all gone after
long decades, houses gone dark, curtainless windows, empty driveway—

fat cats disappear with millions after shanking the economy, thousands
tramping the streets, fruitless, families coming apart nowhere to go. after

painting a ceiling where roof leak burst thru last summer, I sit alone silently
& listen, tender moments passing, ephemeral yet precious after so much

death & sorrow. crossing over, we scatter roses on the river in July where
last year we spread our mother's ashes, just upstream from her old

bedroom, near moraine where I once risked all to save a drowning dog,
clambering across ice & falling in myself, later feted on evening news—

procession of the dead, everyday *dia de muertos*, mother father mentor
brother father of a friend now racing thru my brains, their fragile memory

all that remains—easily scattered, lost, erased to all in deadline
& routine: thus this fierce light raising my eye to this day, this touch.

She

if the path has led thru horrors & I awake to see
my face in the cracked mirror, if I stumble

out of my bed in darkness & am lost in the silver
of the shattered moon, I see now to seek a deeper love

in she I almost lost, in the silence of shared years—she
who sustained me thru my agonies, she who brought me

up short, a nightmare dreamer, wayward child, mancorpse
thrashing with fear of betrayal & abandonment borne

like a poisoned blade thru childhood to middle age—she
who took my pain & gave back unicorn & millefleurs,

the orchid's delicate curved cup, a tender hand for
the foundling raven—& laid them all at my feet as gifts—

she who bore three children & our two lost babes
thru the long dream & struggle of birth, whose groans

brought speaking tongues & bright young eyes
to my life & hers, she who stood by me when another

would've cast me adrift & called out "good riddance,"
she who took my hand & would not let go. I rise today

to sing her praises: she has borne deep memory of
generations coming & going, given language to those

with none, tutored the broken child & raised her up—
skilled gardener training the vine she nurtured to reveal

the passion flower within when none believed it would live,
she who is neither little flower nor rosa mundi but one who'd

sit alone with a lost child & teach her to sing, him to heal
his wounds. grant, you who bear deep love's weight, that such

love must bear us thru all the sorrows we ourselves make,
the wounds for which the springtime balm flows.

April

past blackened ground, ashpiles, twisted red pine boles
scorched yet still alive, miles of cut & sawed trunks, logs
stacked for the trucks to come, brush piles once canopies

swaying in light breeze on a day as blue as this, I wander
to moraine's edge, down thru pinetop juniper balsam
beavercut aspens laid flat or standing in groups, mists

clearing on the river below, down to the good ground.
I'll arrive, journey's end, greet brother & old friends,
stare into campfire ashes where flames lit last night's

madhouse tales: finally, all deaths end for a time:
offload my kayak, clear ground & stake out the tarp,
set up tent & arrange pad, sleeping bag, pillow, camp kit,

moccasins & lantern, notebook & books, unzip windows
lie sideways in shade that I might ascend on currents
racing among high pines oaks & maples, lose myself in

flashing wavelights, hairpin turns, sinkholes, chopwaves
pushing back upriver, thru cedar swamps & past high banks,
to the great lake beyond. now, lie still, listen, let all that go.

The Crippled Doe

dreaming as I rounded
the bend, my paddle still:

a wounded doe
                        staggered into
the stream
crossing—

the wound, fractured thigh or
muscle torn in wild dodge thru trees
(hunters' missed shot?)

seeing me, she turned
frantic, swimming
ahead, ears
            laid back to listen.

I slowed & gave her room,
yet she did not cross, came up

            & hobbled along sand bank
then back into the racing currents,
finally crossing,

standing on the shore—
she did not plunge
into cedars & safety, but
stared directly

in my eyes as I passed, still—

Two for Creeley

For Love

in tears her
marriage in ruins
she poked thru

my books until
lighting on
Creeley's *For*

Love—she'd
take that
& carry it & keep it—

though later
many times she'd
find herself

drunk in a
ditch crying out for
a lover, a place to piss,

heaving toward
some face some
hope for lost love—

these leaves did
see her through
like they say—

words

postcards
scribbled
in haste—

onward,
he would sign,
even to

a great
emptiness—
new

leaves
unfurl in
april sun—

good day
returning to
good earth.

2005, revised 10 December 2021

Blues for Frank

for Frank Salamone (1947-2012)

Young Man Blues

Leaning over the guitar, eyes intent
      on skeletal fingers, strings leaping
           with young man fire & long nights
burning those notes in the blue room

      of dreams, to get past the half moon over
          the broken city, the lost loves, to sing
thru to boom boom dawn running from
      home & somehow find the tune that

         salves the soul & sings free of the many
chains that break us all—taking the dark dream
      within, *living* with it, not denying it,
         when the sky is crying & there's only

a pigfoot & a bottle of beer & a shaking
      money maker to find some way to work
         thru it, transcend it, burnish our hearts
with the suffering none can escape.

The gift taken

When M.S. took his fingers & silenced his guitar,
he sang among blue-gummed Skeletones of providence—
      he sang & would not be still.

Lost to his great gift, he was still able to pluck out
"Camptown Races" on a banjo, that a young girl
      might find a song.

In later years, even as his body curled against him
& left him abed, his angel Fran kept him that he might
      sing & sigh with a friend.

Joining the chorus

Here's to Doehler-Jarvis workers coming home from the long shifts,
to Sicilian beauty and elegance silent presence in every gesture,

here's to Woody Guthrie, to Bobby Dylan, to Spider John Koerner
and Robert Johnson, to Mississippi John Hurt and Doc Watson, to

Son House and Hank Williams, to Bert Jansch and John Renbourn,
to the 10,000 anonymous pickers & singers still in the blue dream,

to Grandma Josie whose recipes Sue learned by watching—
no measurements—to his many loves and his fierce friends,

years of running wild with a harp and a bottle of Southern Comfort,
yakking until 3 a.m., passing out and yakking again, with no

particular place to go and no end in mind—his old National Steel
& Martin guitars weathered classics silent, still now—now he's

free in the rent party rag wang-dang-doodle where all careless
loves now rest, no police dog blues, hellhounds sighing beneath

the table with hambones and the wild women singing like Bessie
in every kitchen—let the freight train rolling thunder midnight

special wail down those tracks, trumpets blasting out every window,
free now in the blue chorus of wailing angels, free picking free

when the last deal's gone down and where indeed we shall not be
moved, not be moved, not be moved, hang it on the wall, brother.

American Pewter with Burroughs II:
Green is a Man / To Fill is a Boy

Robert Rauschenberg riffs on two lines by William S. Burroughs

1.
The green man leafy head in hands comes back again & again:
I remember Billy, son, scapegoat, burdened with the life he found:

cirrhotic, bleeding out his esophagus, finally in hepatic coma,
"swimming up" to his eyes from within to observe bleak cartoon

figures going thru motions in the room beyond—saved only
when others bardo-prayed he'd go to the light, his father drove them

away—"Dammit, he's in a fucking coma and he might listen!"
Billy—who bade "all trees & true persons the clearest of futures."

2.
Greek warriors lean together, flowing beards curling hair, fierce eyes
intent on battle to come, another battle. Sappho lamented such
beauty one sees in faces like these, marching to war, full of high

phrases, valorous tongues, arms bristling with arms, killers with
faces of angels—Sappho, who cried out to Anaktoria that her footstep,
the light in her eyes set her heart thrumming more strongly than
                    all armed killers others might sing.

3.
The ironworker spread-eagled high above the city, his billed cap cocked
like a *statement* atop his head, walks skyward, free, beyond earthbound spirits
trapped in the squalor of watches & traffic, appointments, briefcases loaded

with the flotsam of routine—imagine him now, naked to the world, human
form at last, swinging in heights above, godlike, filled as a boy is filled
                    to be a man, to green as an earth in season.

For Antler, after the storm

after whiteouts & deep freeze, the moon hangs above mounds & river,
currents move beneath ice jams & broken trunks, traffic racing beyond—
on Madeleine Island elder ghosts shape birch & pine craft to cross waves,

spirit an old woman to sundown, last ripples before the moon, still mirror
where faces stare back in the dark: for Antler has paused to sing the last
elegiac lullaby for she who bore him to this life, hand tenderly pulling aside

aging tresses that she might see the clear day. silent hours pass & still he is
beside her in her calm passage, even his poems flown beyond him now, still
in back pockets of coast-bound boys, in the hands of he who dreams he'll

strike a pose atop El Capitan, who strips naked & worships the sun atop
Audubon, those racing to the wild side for succor, attuned to the elder
murmur along the silent path now become Broadway, Mannahatta. still

the poet passes the night, pausing only to share sighs with his other side,
lifelong love, Jeff who faced down Death & sang the tale. still his hand
clasps his mother's in Time's sureness, dreams that once bore flesh,

the childhood song that promises light in shimmering lake & waves—
        sing softly in his honor, her honor, under the moon
                by the great lake's shore.

Thornapple

my mother disappeared
in swirling waves

as children and friends
poured her ashes

into the river near her
old bedroom window

my sister reached into the bag
& scattered the last ashes

across the water, slapped
her hands together,

dust flying out: wild rose
on the high bank beyond.

So the day begins

hour of the silent lapping waves,
stillness of the reeds in the cove—
last stars still bright
& the fading moon still bright.
far away, the others sleep.

I sit, breathing in quiet rhythm, awaiting
the day's fire, the rising winds,
the waves slashing the breakwater,
thunderous,
gulls still above riding the winds,
searching, searching.
I stand & turn on my heel,
bowing in the four directions.

may dreams pass thru this day
evaporating or
passing my ken or desire.
let my friends awake now:
their voices bring us all to laughter.

The Gateless Gate 2014-2016

I, You, She or He

for Jaume Plensa

three dreamers sit together on green, grown
yet coyly clasping hands below knees—
facing each other like lovers, emergent as

hollow, their flesh & form become shining
letters in patterns where once words became
the lines by which they measured lives, words

which became them. manitou winds blow
softly thru leaves, thru vacant heads & torsos,
lips still forming sighs lost forever—they

might have danced in starlit nights or sang
heartsongs for lost love, as if they live still
in visions & sighs now lost to a generation

racing to its own dead ends. now silence
fills the green where a distant child's echoing
song is lost in one horizon-bound jet trail,

where the dreamers sit in stasis: we three
too have come to look back at them, animated
in our conversation, lost already in memory.

A Language of Our Time

Hanneke Beaumont at the Gardens

gaunt
                    face
trapped in
the gaze, steady, vacant yet curious,
claylike,
          moving yet still—
as if reaching for *something*
                    lost—some
melancholy,
pensive, eyes staring into *yours*,
                              deeply—

she is sometimes two—
staring back at her other self
she,
          wordless
                              still
in a landscape where
                    cars & busses, harried
pedestrians pass,
                    staring
in the endless honking
sorrow of
routines not their own.
                              they stretch
          to speak
a language—
          intense,
                    unheard.

Le Départ

each devours the other's last glance—caught in her other
self, identical as doppelgangers in stasis, slowly turning away—

she turns to the racing crowds, to the rush hour streets beyond,
breathless at last on the stair and up to their tiny apartment,

half-empty demitasses still on the table, the bowl of fruit, silence
and solitude of the fourth floor window, and beyond the window

rows of identical windows, roofs, traffic, the river in the distance,
trees bent in the wind, sailboats tacking in the heavy swells—

her other self turns to the sleepy agent taking tickets, stolid guard,
the echoing walk down the chute to the faux smiles of attendants,

the pilot turning to the cockpit, the roar of take-off, and now clouds,
the little window with its parade of visions, the vast blue beyond.

one lies
prone,
head resting on bent arm,
legs extended—
the face
expressionless.
behind this
                    staring
          silence,
another sits, turned away,
bent
          forward,
                              grim
as the darkness beyond

Connected and Disconnected

she is wiping her hands on a rag,
staring down at her companion,

who sits—hands grasping her dress,
eyes cast down, counting the seconds.

a third sits nearby, she too gazing
down on the one. She is caught

in their gaze, in the silent moment
the two share in their implacable

stare, each unaware of the other in
the intensity of their gaze on *her.*

another steps gingerly on a pedestal,
stepping
            forward,
                        struggling
                                    to keep
balance. quiet day in the city,
            pedestrians
stepping
            forward
                        behind, unseeing,
            their dreams
submerged elsewhere, their
                        tongues
            silent,
                        a language without
shape or sound,
trapped on the lips, in the eyes.

Wyrd Song

blinding fog over the great lake's waters, the ship plowing thru
& I, at 66, dream with a boy's anxieties—the rusty freighter

ghost ship emerging from nowhere, shattering the side, the roll
& plunge through 900 feet of water to the bottom littered with

flotsam, centuries of traffic & tragedy scattered everywhere—
now, a month later, after a great storm & sundown's shining light,

I lie in my bedroom with Denise Levertov's "Staying Alive,"
wondering how we all survived the *sturm und drang* of those years.

the night is quiet. I have read too many screeds by elders lamenting
their years, full of aching regrets. We have all been fools at one time

or another. I have survived & know illumination unseen by youth,
gifts I could not have found before; the lake journey was a glass

showing the unseeable shore, when one gropes toward light, yet
crowds of lovers & friends greeted us there, the sky clearing—

so this present journey demands a finer craft, an ear more tuned
to the voices in the silence, a grasp of the runes in stones where

the old ones walked as this land & sea were yet untouched
& dew was on the long grass under summer's full honey moon.

Early Spring Morn Milwaukee

1.

Antler's upstairs caring for Jeff—
lung infection, with endless barrage

pills & injections, struggles to stand,
pillows for bony buttocks when he sits.

sunshine floods down in brisk air,
light wind moving spruce & cedar

branches, emerging tulips, violets, lilies
& in the park on the hill beyond,

a robust young man swings again &
again, driving baseballs into the cage.

it is a difficult time. Antler descends &
sits with me. we speak of native glyphs

north of Superior—sacred ground, sign
& instruction for those who arrive—

the faces of Pompeii looking back at us,
ancestral faces reaching thru time, haunted—

the eagle that flew low over Sue's head
in Betsie River sunshine: aged

Ojibwe, hearing this, raised his eyes,
saying "that is a very good sign."

2. On the Milwaukee River Trail

as Antler & I make our way on the old trail
Jeff fought to preserve in public forum, decades
facing off with developers & politicians,

now bright yellow-green leaved trees greet us
in their springtime dresses—ducks & ducklings,
garter snakes sunning themselves, & hikers'

kind halloos. we wander, talking the boy-love
of Shakespeare's sonnets, older men who need
young friends not for sex but shared affection,

shared experiences, Diotima's advice, the scene
where young Maurice in oral translation class
is admonished to omit the passage with

the "unspeakable vice of the Greeks." we are
old friends on this May morn at the bright river,
friendly young boys passing us on the trail, lusty

hunks practicing ball in the park above, & I
dream of mound builders who must have walked
these paths before Marquette & Joliet passed thru,

of Margaret Fuller in her tour of the lakes,
noting the lives of women in this frontier city,
of the history of mills & factories, sewer overflow,

now in spring sun the river come back to shine
in our eyes & in those we meet. fine day indeed,
to hike together, wander, & dream of many loves.

Adieu à Jeff Because

Sun flooded skies above gnarled peaks as we hiked
Fourth of July trail to the Continental Divide, boys
now loose after ecopoetics rain dance rendezvous,

sharing our love on a narrow trail thru switchbacks,
past meadow-bright columbines where avalanches
once shattered stands of spruce, broken timber

now in valleys below. Brothers, we shared silence
& laughter in the crispness of clear air among peaks,
our dreams aired out, wild syllables over the divide—

I like to think of Jeff now as he & Antler stood
along the trail, their shared smiles, ecstatic that they
could hike this land together, as they did thru life.

His environmental jeremiads, songs awake to silent
heron, butterfly wing, tamarack, swamp & dell where
Gaia sleeps, now speak as Muir & Leopold spoke—

he & lifelong lover Antler showed a jaded world
a love so tender yet potent through cancers, lost
parents, a thousand heartbreaks—firm through all.

Silence now along the river trails in blue moonlight,
genial halloos at dawn beneath singing canopies,
quiet splash in lapping waves he defended for decades.

Dawn Kayaking the Owashtanong

for Curt Jordan

1.
this sunrise
                              flashes
            down the river

dreamscape
mythos these decades,
manitous

                  among the Mounds
in gnarled woods,
            ancient ponds & streams,

despite the occasional oil well
sucking
life blood of the land &

                  long played-out
gypsum mines
where dust-covered workers

            slaved & paid & died on stoops,
trains showering sparks
                  thru the elder quiet.

now we are
                  fully
awake, alive
on the shining skin
                  of the waters,
                              clouds reflected

skyward, disturbed only
as we pull

        upriver, as

voyageurs & Anishinaabe
did in dreamtime,
silent as the sun tops the trees—

       herons overhead,
fish
sliding beneath us as ever.

2.

though we do not speak
       of your grandfather's passing,
he is

with us this morning,
elder spirit
       observing our talk, when

we are moved to talk.
       changes are of course
a part of the journey,

as when we rounded a bend
       & came up on Heron Island.
the year after
a great ice jam
slammed crashing
         fallen tree trunks

bent & shattered
into the west flank

of the stream around the island—
you worked
in among the trunks,
                    the flow still moving
slowly amid
splintered detritus,
& there you found

nesting herons nervous with chicks.
this year,
the streambed was filled in,

sand & earth
                    deposits,
                            the island now

a part of the shore,
subsumed.
                    herons arrow

down the river,
as do those
who have left us

still.

Rix is Gone

Bobby Rix has died, wild Irish Bobby,
mainstay WFMU Rix Mix DJ, *Boardwalk*
poet of quick clear portraits: his mother's

matchmaking, the burglar, the landlord
& fix-it Louie, his father's life as reenactor,
the ballet receptionist, his Nana—his

60th birthday wish to me lament we
couldn't end with a Sandy Hook sunset
or a carousel ride at Seaside Heights—

who sent me the tightest pure New Jersey
celebrations of Italian ices, Betty Boop,
lovers under the boardwalk, long beach

that gave generations their adult eyes,
yet also no-truck vision of polluters,
corrupt politicians, industrial horrors.

Bobby & James showed me Asbury Park
Madame Marie's, Bill Williams' Great Falls—
the still-racing baseball players, the old

woman in red-trimmed peasant black,
the falls themselves descent beckoning
as the ascent beckoned. Bobby Rix is gone—

home to join his Nana, Rix, who chose
his friends carefully, chose me & kept me
 all these years.

End at the beginning

for Johnny B

crisp bright August sunshine, light breezes in the pines & birches—
I pass over the decades we shared, the agonies and wild highs

of a lifetime, struggle with the face in the mirror, long days & nights'
hard labor & lost hopes, the days passing like clouds, & tho the tale

is long, one returns at last to the beginning, where hope & despair
are not yet the measures of the heart: wild boys racing into the deep

country on fast wheels, voyageurs paddling upstream to the deep
woods where the ruined cabin, its roof fallen in, gave us dreams of

other lives gone this way, imagining their own escapes—& we,
naked in moonlight, the juice of stolen raspberries on our chins,

howling with wine & cigarettes, little saw nor cared what lay ahead.
our own cabin fires warmed us against winter winds, we raised a glass

in the brief light. Time & the world would bend us soon enough—
yet these days define the fires that made us what we are & were.

the grief is measureless, so deep that words cannot fully tell the tale,
yet this is what we were, what makes us still, even beyond the grave.

The Gateless Gate

Four stood together
among ancient cedars,
maples still dormant,

rows of graves laid out
down the hill before them,
the busy traffic beyond—

a simple service, then
seeing into each other's
eyes, rolling clouds above.

May Song

flowering plum petals blow across the yard
as white dogwood blooms unfold and open.

the river has returned to its banks, deer prints
saunter thru mud and shallow pools to the beach.

among bushes wavering in the spring breeze,
an oriole clings to its slender branch, eyeing me.

rangers cut only branches crossing the path
of beaver-felled aspen. beaver will need the rest.

I cut dead trunks & limbs from the witch hazel.
now she dances with new growth in the breeze.

last year's redbud trunks died in winter freeze;
tiny leaves and stems spring anew from roots.

sunset is fierce yellow through cedar branches.
songs fade to silence in the campfire's last coals.

The Work

the fisherman's bike lies
where it fell. He is
quick to cast his line.

cormorants fly low,
searching the dark water.
the swan is still

on her nest. how many
times have I rounded
this corner, racing

to the hill beyond,
blind to bright
shine on the waves?

soon I'll be home,
survey the garden where
my rough boots will

tramp, where I'll kneel
& plant golden zinnias,
heliotrope, red geraniums,

same early summer winds
caressing my skin & cheeks,
the work *still* before me.

"the weight of the world is love"

after the Charleston 9,
        gunned down in prayer
even as they shared Love,

after care came for the poor,
        the needy, in spite of the rage
of rich men's puppets,

after marital bliss so long
        denied, the doors opened
the business of liberty

unfinished still, after
        all this, & that great amazing
grace come down on us all,

tonight, tonight
        Venus & Jupiter come together
& fire the sky, together.

Leaves in Fall

Sit quietly:
falling
white pine needles,

maples,
river birch, gingko,
oak and redbud leaves

shelter this land
thru the long winter.
hollies and crabapple

shine in harsh light,
loaded with red berries,
still beauties in

earth's turn
toward deep
snows, whipping

winds.
—rest now,
be kind.

long thin clouds

for Wang Ping

bluish grey streaks in the sky of light
blinding fog banks below
then the lake, the Wisconsin shore—

descending to Chicago, Alex somewhere
in one of those buildings below—
voices snarling & cajoling on screens—

beyond this window seat, looking away
to what dreams may come at wing tips—
Siberian & Californian methane floods,

bleeding eyes and limbs after barrel bombs,
beheadings, terror attacks, quakes,
bombs bombs bombs still raining down—

a city poisoned, a prayer, a hope denied,
a quiet song garbled on the lips—
Sue, I placed a white dahlia card on your desk

for your waking moments—
Jim, I send vajras that you might heal,
James, may you rise from your bed

& host that Jersey City series,
Antler, I send you a lake brother's kiss—
Ping, warm sunny afternoon at your table,

silence in your kitchen,
white prayer flags beyond your window
 wave in the breeze.

For Anne at 70

today winds battered old growth oaks,
       split aging boughs from trunks—
              crashing, *thumping* across wilderness,

              in the swamplands and along banks
       thru this darkness of mounds &
manitous, the voices singing within.

I thought of you at 70, all the mornings
       rising to teach, to read, to catch another
              flight, surrounded by young poets looking

              for visions, intense in listening, quiet
       the first time I met you—mobbed by
hysterical TAs *wanting* answers NOW—

your calm undisturbed, picking and
       choosing responses, that quiet sureness
              becoming theirs in the sunlit moment.

I remember too that ferocious
       crack in the world torrent of
              words on fire, syllables crackling

              in the audience's ears in a basement
       bookstore reading in Boulder,
or amazed on a Lake Michigan shore

looking across to horizon line
       beyond which Milwaukee must be—
              "this is no lake—it's an inland sea!"

then too you rescued Jim in his lost dream,
came to Morgan when she lost Chris,
quiet kindness measured to their needs.

now seven decades on, now
the wise elder shepherd to flocks of
crazed poets, dreamers with fists of angst,

you remain a signal bearer of light
in this opening Kali Yuga, heart
daughter and mother, seer, prophet,

good friend who graced others with
kindness. as I pass millennial
mounds, oak boughs tossing above,

great blow downriver where a fisherman's
craft is buffeted toward rocks & fallen
timbers, I pause at the bridge to bow

in four directions & push off for
swan ponds & herds of leaping deer,
giving thanks for your touch, in memory,

in the patterns of my own life.
quiet heart's peace, Anne,
you've earned it, earned

love of peers, the yet-to-be
scribed songs of the untamed heart.

Minneapolis Airport Delay

Sitting among passengers more disgruntled than I,
I navigate the ghost landscape of the tale I once dreamed
we knew, now littered with shattered cities—O Aleppo,

streets of many colors, intricate designs, lush plantings
now reduced to blackened rubble, bombed-out roofs,
windowless streets gaping like so many dead dreams—

in America, black men shot to death almost daily by
frenzied cops, and in downtown Dallas, cops under fire,
open carry macho men running away like chickens—

here the nightly news replays too: the dead president,
the pistol-splattered Vietnamese man, brains shot to oblivion,
rise anew, the silence carrying off babes never to be born.

now the republican convention drones on elevated TVs,
speaker after speaker hissing into the aether, slamming fists,
anxious passengers around me trying to ignore the vicious

messages & angry gestures, the cheering well-fed white
people in their tailored suits & dresses. Delays confirmed:
I should make Phoenix by 12:30 mountain time, wandering

in a dream under the haze of a desert moon. barely miles
from here, the Castile family struggles to bury their son,
killed by cops for a dead taillight and an honest response:

friends and neighbors unable to speak, left with empty hands,
eyes red, torn hearts—we in this airport fools of Time,
waiting in this howling sorrow trapped in anxious silence.

The Train: *Howl* in Chicago

for Alex and her students

". . . a situation so surrealistic and hallucinatory and violent
that there could be no outcome but some massive nervous
breakdown in America when people find out that they've
not only been lied to but drawn into a dream of reality
which is not only false but painful and murderous . . .
I shuddered, realizing that America was taking a fall, was
going to have to take a big fall."
                                —Allen Ginsberg,
                                from an interview
                                by James McKenzie (1978)

Prologue

Amtrak to the city by the Lake, I'll teach *Howl* to Alex's students,
 guessing if the great poem might speak to them in their
teenage skins, so many nightmares gone down the mad sewer
 since Allen's trial & vindication, & now a nation careening
toward disasters—recalling my own youthful determination to learn
 the lexicon of this prophecy, read its voice aloud, any students
now persistent, finding the vision among teenage fears & sorrows?
 memories of Allen & Dick Gregory leading protesters away
as cops rioted, bashing the brains of children, dragging them from
 Grant Park to jail, 1968, & of Allen reading to overflow crowd,
Hill Auditorium, Moratorium Day, *Howl* singing thru the horror
 of those days, bringing so many to tears at last after friends dead
in Nam, others come home with hell in their own minds.

Kalamazoo Station thru the farmlands

Reading—Allen in Prague, the new "open consciousness," human
to human, friendly, Kral Majales, notebooks stolen, "bougerant!"—
the prophet hustled out of the country—what open consciousness
survives in this angry age, who can speak for those lost, in sorrow,
struggling to find a life, love, dreams shared now?

train pulls thru vistas of farmland, scrub oaks & dogwoods still
clinging to last year's now-whited leaves, flooded swamplands,
racing thru small towns—workers' houses, flashing lights,
old woman in babushka waiting patiently with her cane,

now deep woodlands thousands of trees lit by new spring sun,
then deep fogs, a whole world gone white-out, shapes like ships
barely visible, now emerging to sunlight again—
300 acre fields already plowed, black loam where some farmer,
wife or kid steered tractor & disks thru a vacant afternoon
dreaming to early sunset, eagles riding winds above.

Mind jumps the tracks—yesterday, Comey & Rogers sat before
the committee, an administration awash in its lies, British howling
"ridiculous" to lame claims, shy German reporter now a hero
at home, putting Trump in fury of his own blame-shifting,
half-forgotten North Koreans plotting to blow us all to hell,
Russians secretly cracking up at this circular knife-dance in
Washington, Barnum & Bailey gone ape in the "hallowed halls"—

turkeys in corn stubble second field over, sun still a heart's candle,
a white horse alone in a meadow lifts her head to watch us pass.

Michigan City to Calumet, on to Gary

Gas & coal plant—looks like a nuke—exhaust plume
 blows up to the sky, marina's dockmen & boaters scurry
among newly placed boats, gigantic factories corrode
 into the polluted landscape where nothing grows, smoke still
spewing from endless stacks, rivers & streams metallic grey-blue
 green or yellow, laced with decades of chemicals,
piles of refuse dumped into the dying landscape, miles of stunted
 & dying trees, branches broken off as in Dante's hell, naked
earth, not even a wisp of grass or bush—where'd our dream of
 waking consciousness, kindness, Gaia respect, diamond-hard
compassion go? Allen joked he'd be in a cottage 20 years after
 Howl, with wife & 12 kids—what humor led him from prophecy
to meditation on train tracks to dreamtime in sacred rocks?
 I dream of Blake singing on his deathbed, Albion's glad day boy
still. Out the window again—warehouses & gas works, tough men
 grinding thru the day, machines roaring in still air, loading,
unloading trucks, wasteland with no sunflowers nor mimosas—
 Bobby Rixon, your poems of gas works & delicate fields
struggling to flower haunt me still.

Yes I built that cabin above the river, mad skinny sixteen year old,
 & we sang "Fern Hill" with our youths' dying breaths, drunk
in the stolen hours—I muse that youthful dreams fleet like
 last season's flocks, cannot sustain one in the floods of
child-changing time, today's dream become tomorrow's cast-off
skin in the endless charade of the self—yet honor it as that face
that got us thru in the endless dying days.

Still the sunlight.

Union Station: waiting out the time

Black child in your gold-sequined coat, how many years hence
will you recall this coat, this day when your mom took you
on the train, showed us all that you'll be a goddess child,
 your smile already flashing?

Browned white oak leaf on the blackened walkway, tracks 18-20,
how'd you get here among motorized carts & jostling new arrivals?

Amish men in broad-brimmed black hats dark clothes long beards
stand in the Great Room, anxious, hanging together looking
out at others, plainly themselves in this seemingly alien world—
the women join them, nunlike dark blue dresses & white caps,
children around them laughing, conscious only of adventure.

A Howling Time

The students—quick, aware, yet unsure how to read the poem—
we speak of standing for one's own, as Allen did
during Grant Park police riots, the courage to keep mantric calm—
for me, the losses in Nam, 200 dead boys each week,
childhood friend Chris, machine gunned on his first recon mission
& we, walking up the hill in tears, in chilling rain—
those returned trapped in memory, recalling Bill Shields' poem of
car backfire, his hands killing VC—on his own child's throat—
my Bosnian student's fierce insistence on telling her best friend's
story—raped by gangs, her body found by UN peacekeepers—
wanting it published—"Americans *need* to know these things."
Alex's students are moved, partly aware today too
is a howling time—Trump's OK to pollute streams after decades
of cleanup, the Lakes under threat, line 5 debacle-to-be,
Standing Rock protests for sacred ground cleared off for pipeline,
mosques burned, threats to Jewish community centers,
gravestones kicked over & sprayed with swastikas, Mexican
families fearful of deportation squads, children torn
from parents, debacles unfolding from Europe to North Korea,
Russia & Syria, the lamp at the golden door suddenly dark—
this litany's a journey of sorrow & rage in the "land of the free,"
    yet "the world won't change by hiding from it"—
thus "best minds" are "starving, hysterical, naked" still.

The Dream

The youthful face
in the cabin window,

hawk in the high pine
shaken loose in fierce winds,

now diving riverward where
the silent woman weeps

among great oaks
on the ancient path—

the hawk now skimming
along water's roiled mirror—

gone.

That face in the cabin window
now floating across memory

to another face, a dawn,
a dream yet mirage.

Monroe to Canal on Foot

Off the red line, mammoth buildings shoulder each other
 so many swollen egos, tyrannical breast-beating in stone,
commuters race the lights, crowds trapped crossing or staring
 blankly at crosswalks—white men in striped business suits
march to their different drummer, so many tanks headed
 to a burning battlefield—their Private Bank, their
                    Asphyxiation Bank—
laughing workers in yellow safety vests inflate a 10 ft plastic rat,
 bloody mouth facing the ravenous traffic,
strike signs lifted in the morning melée. I ask for a photo—
 "I was a union man back when!" and then—

the river itself, hemmed in by behemoths—yet still the river,
same river where Marquette spent days awaiting winter's end
among the Illinois, en route to the Kaskaskians where he'd
preach his last sermon to hundreds, his health already failing,
then heading north along Michigan's shores, dunes & forests
where death took him on the sandy shores near Ludington.

turn left at Canal, on to Union Station Cathedral of Commerce,
 Midwest crossroad where I'll sit three hours, finish
Howl *on Trial*, Mike Schumacher's new *First Thought*,
 dream the time, call Alex to say I placed her key, thanks,
call Sue to say I'll be home soon, missing her though exhilarated,
 good to go on foot, my last foray, most intimate gaze & dream
in the city of big shoulders. board my train, hail & farewell!

The Blue Room of Dreams 2017-2023

Kali Yuga Super Blue Blood Moon

vicious politicians, screams all across our sorry old globe, yet
tonight is a still moon, stars and clouds flung across aether,
my shadow moving on the snowshine, in trees, on the river,
as in my childhood and in frozen camp as a young man—

musing beyond destroyed families, bombed communities,
spectres of Mammon & Moloch marching across the planet—
O silence in the inner ear and in that sanctum within where
thought dissolves—I have always leapt like a glad day boy,

arriving in the promised jeweled light, each instant split into
fleeting, shining facets, tender beyond hope, beyond dream,
even in this elder age where the cloud of thought vanishes
at the beckoning grave, the cave where the child still dreams

days ahead balancing on shoots breaking the soil to new life.
the heart's caught in the hare's leap, the deeper breath—
light the lamp with your shaky hand, old man, and sing.
the hopeful day has not yet come, the calm fleeting dawn.

The Mountain: Inauguration 2017

"the weight we carry . . . is love."
—Allen Ginsberg

As many hearts many tongues raise their voices
in the Standing Rock dawn,
frozen wildlands attacked by oil company thugs
posing as lawmen,
as women warriors board planes, buses, load cars
to make themselves heard in the din,
hatefilled hissing poseurs and a man grinding his teeth
& snarling at the whole world,

my heart is a mountain
lost in storms & a wilderness of sighs, yet
these First People, these women teach us
 to stand—
for sacred land, signs in the turning day
& the million stars,
a handshake & signature not swept away by time,
a clean future not poisoned by black gold,
living waters flowing free to the mother of waters,
hands reaching to those unable to help themselves,

the immigrant who dreams a new dream,
memory of millions come here for refuge,
for the lamp by the golden door,
lives packed in suitcases, tongues
bringing new accents,
sorrows borne in silence finally spoken aloud.

The mountain is still there.
The moon awaits our gaze.

Fragile Moves

She wrote, asking
how to face deep
sorrow, intense

regrets, how write
thru them, free
her heart. Stung by

unquiet recall, I too
struggled in dreams,
kept my silence yet

did penance in my
own way, but how
give advice to another,

even a dear friend?
I reach for the right
word, looking into

her eyes and wishing
her only the most
freeing of thoughts,

aware too of the
fragile moves
that keep a boat

upright in a storm,
seeking quiet waters,
calm shores.

Flight to Paumanok: A Still Station

JFK full stop—50 mph winds, gusting
even higher over NYC, swirling—
we deplane at Detroit, city of my birth—

airline agent beleaguered & bullied,
irate passengers wanting answers, *now*—
arms gesticulating, faces contorted.

others phone those they love, lament
missed connections, or watch the slow
rolling clouds, bright light & horizon

with its promise. a still station now.
fellow passengers share tales as I
outline Walt's endlessly rocking

cradle, the bird's lament that gave him
his calling, life of singing words as
comfort in this sea of sorrow, even as

I too am headed for his Paumanok,
where I'll share hours with old friends,
make new ones. I'll sing my poems,

recitative in East Setauket & Garden City,
visit Whitman birthplace & wonder how
the Walt Whitman Mall across the street

might sit with him in these latter days
when the heart itself is a commodity—
I hear the mourning bird in the swamp

even as the agent announces we'll
take off in an hour, ah generous
spirit of singing words abiding still.

Manhattan from Jersey City

Early morning sunlight in the park,
looking thru haze over the river
to Manhattan, Allen's "Man City,

my city," later the horror of falling
towers, murdered thousands, I
marvel at the city now reborn,

boats on the river below, busy
unseen folk striding in labors.
How does a city resurrect itself

after such destruction, and we,
aging daily through the cycles
of time, how confront the changes

in our public lives. James and I
share a coffee with younger poets
in a shop beyond the park, amazed

at their new visions, their kindnesses,
a key for later Fox & Crow recitative
with old friends and new, true

to ourselves, glad to share this space,
hear our shared voices rising above
sorrows and memory-sustaining love.

After the Polar Vortex

Shoveled the driveway clean
final double check
visa application
supporting documents
passport
off to bed, asleep as I hit the pillow—
wake late out the door
bare knuckles on icy roads
to the train, the train

ah
in my seat soft breath soft light
no destination
only wait & ride

Strange, taking in familiar streets & woods
from upper deck window in the dark—
now
freight yards, acres of junked cars
snow-covered, hoods up

& beyond,
streets whose rhythms I've known intimately,
barely visible
headlights unseen drivers
bare-knuckles on wheel
tense, struggling in snow piles
& shiny layers of ice
here
traffic light signaling the road to home,
Suzy asleep in her bed
still,

Will laboring over
the rising action of his second novel
one light still on over his computer.

On to Holland, where the train will fill, then
to Chicago consulate on Erie Street, now
blasting thru the dark.
                              I dream of Beijing,
Chengdu where Du Fu built his thatched refuge,
found brief respite from endless war in bright mornings,
garden and quiet evenings driven out by yet another revolt,
another invasion—

even as I roll across the yet unknown
landscapes & wild skies to Suining,
home of Guan Yin and Chen Zi'ang.

May I make this journey with dignity and grace,
may I honor my poems and the poems of friends,
make new friends, sing & laugh together.
Let me honor the spirit of my nation and my people,

sit humbly in the halls and gardens of ancient China,
honor her people and her ancestors.
Let us enter a whole new world with open eyes & ears,
a clear heart, as father Whitman once did.

First streak of deep red along the horizon,
below deep whitish blue billows
echoing deep blue-white of snowy fields,
one farmhouse light almost at the horizon.

White woods in the valley below,
rising to hills above, now a great pond icy sheet
rimmed with brush, what spirits must be waking

here to struggle through another day?
What eyes watch us pass,
even in the depths of deep forest
or in the workers' paradise kitchen window?
Jet passes overhead, sleepers
headed who knows where?

What wranglings, desires, dreams
& great extended conversations,
notes tapped out with tenuous fingers,
far above us here?

The Moon

tonight, the full moon lights the snowy forest,
still blue dream beyond hope, beyond sorrow.

his memorials for harmony ignored again and again,
Chen Zi'ang spent a night with an old friend talking
mountains, streams, his coming journey to Loyang,
this night's deep bonds memorials to one he might
never see again—the road leading forever away.

Du Fu found a dream refuge in his thatched hut,
despite poverty, free of slavish work, among family
and friends—yet endless wars and rebellions
drove him off. clinging to a single twig, only
moonlight over waters shaped his long journey.

Waiting for dawn in a Beijing hotel room

Capitol airport lines
like JFK's though more quiet, orderly—
helpful airport cop showed me how to find taxi exit,
taking airport shuttle train to the end of the line—
thinking of Du Fu, his many regrets & melancholy
as invaders closed in on his thatched sanctuary,
though he could still find the silences.
We all have regrets, rethinking earlier choices,
behaviors, losses
as we age, yet there is a silent space for those
limping toward death,
a quiet dance with each moment, and I despite myself
am giddy as a schoolboy in love
to be opening my eyes to a nation of great landscapes,
history and culture,
a people moving quickly into this century,
kids full of life—
a young mother who'd talked with me
in Chicago as we waited for our plane,
the concerns for her child in these early years,
bringing her teething child aboard a 13 hour flight
alone, pleased to be heard.

From the top step of Guangde Temple

Suining rests in its lotus cradle of wetlands,
among blue mountains beyond mountains,

Guan Yin's poured waters in streams & passing
clouds, a stillness for the beating heart.

Chen Zi'ang saw the shattered bones of warriors,
sorrows of court & commoners, stood fast

for harmony, wept at the losses & sought refuge.
now, a grizzled old man scratches his head

on the bridge over Fujian River, traffic races
changing lights, horns frantic & restless, yet

at the shrine, a small boy helps his grandpa lift
a frail leg over the high doorway, poets drink

from the sacred well—aged monk hammers
the dharma fish, echoing through the centuries.

March 5 2019; revised Feb. 2021

A Song for Our Lady

for Jacqueline Jung

Here the billowing smoke & flames,
the falling spire, the shrieking crowd—
here the hopes, prayers of generations,
gnarled hands whose gifts built this
sacred dream alive in their voices—

now it is like loved ones lost, a prayer
above all religion, statecraft, economics,
material life, *still* in the feast of fools,
the bells, the hopes of a suffering people,
still center point of a nation, its headless

kings recrowned, gargoyles over the city,
dreamed angels above the endless sighs.
Here gigantic timbers from forests long gone
burned in a moment, gone craftsmen & masons
laboring thru centuries to give faces to mercy,

vanished, even the armies of firemen sweating
thru this night to head off the flames, saving
the great stone walls and flying buttresses,
testament of hope returning even in the dark
as plain folk gather and sing as they have

always gathered, sing for restoration, sing
as sparks fly up over the river and the city,
sing in the tears of those across the world,
sing for unborn generations and those still
in dreams, sing for the returning dawn.

Memory's Balm

the river of my childhood, wellspring of memory—
first day of the recent floods, we had to pull our way

through rabid currents on Tom's homemade rafts
along guy lines to his island home—this visit with

dear friends I'd not seen in decades, siblings to
friends who left too early in lives lost in promise.

Time had divided survivors thru much of our lives,
yet these starshot moments shone with shared

blood and memory. the river raged on in dark
night as we took the rafts shoreward, dreaming

the savage loss, the silent years, memory's balm.
here a lonesome farewell and thankful heart,

here the wistful mind in hazy late night calm,
the still thought, slow unfolding red dawn.

Beyond the dream, the open door

despite the stroke, dreams & memory are intact.
blind in one eye, nearly deaf, he weighs a hard choice:

burial with wife, family or with brothers-in-arms.
he looks up into his visitors' eyes: lived memories

vivid as blood jerk him awake by night, haunt him
still. he has never spoken of this, would forget if he

could, despite the years behind—a kind man, good
husband, good father, helpless as his grown children

watch over his last days. Roses he tended as emblems
of his love, the cabin once his refuge—all now awash

in lost time: clocks striking dead-march hours, lost
friends, loves beyond the dream, the open door.

Among the best minds of his generation

musicians, poets, fiction writers,
actors, all in their mid-twenties,
testified to his touch as they
struggled with his overdose, their

demons, tears and rage. later, I sigh
nightlong all my youthful deaths:
the loss of childhood friend Chris—
machine gunned in Vietnam,

best friend Todd, plane crash in fog,
only his tattooed hand left as ID,
wild poet Chris's heroin overdose:
I felt them around me in darkness.

the cloud only departed at dawn,
the sorrow unnerving, palpable
even as these brilliant youths I saw
were lost, flailing as we had been,

not to be touched, trapped in wild
tears, hearts ablaze in endless sighs.

A Desperate Mother

almost in tears after hours in stores with empty
shelves, empty coolers—no milk for her babes,

no toilet paper nor wipes after fearful hoarders had
grabbed everything and run for the registers.

The old man could not help, suggested she return
in the morning when the store restocks shelves—

"come early" while these others sleep. In the morning
he returned for his own distilled water and milk,

the shelves restocked, he wondering how she'd
gotten through the night, if she'd found her way.

Unbidden dream: a melancholy evening, calm and free

I must speak of the insistent melancholy of age, regrets
lurking behind shared laughter, endless smiles.

my small boat lingers in the eddies, among still waters
moved only by perch fanning slowly in shallows—I lift

my head and see the blue heron above, ancient presence.
the seasons roll on, the sun, now obscured, now the moon,

the body falling apart, gradually shutting down, memory's
tales unfolding like quick films from another life, moments

rising to feverish yet near-silent crescendo, shared warmth
in a friend's touch, radiant eyes lingering in dream. I pass

thru an open door in moonlight, among stars, and leave
the grave to grave business. Dawn comes quickly, I send

blessings for Zhang, wherever he may be now, his last
message speaking of high blood pressure and creatinine,

now prolonged silence after completing his life's work,
dear friend singing quietly beyond the dynamo of dreams.

I am indeed surrounded by spirits day and night, old
loves still palpable, present, as are the sorrows, regrets,

filling the many paths with unheard silences among
the busy living with their chatter and deadlines.

tonight, my kousa flowers fully, as Allen's did in years
after he passed, and the clematis, which struggled

years to simply climb in the orchid porch doorway,
now frames it with wild, open purple flowers: here

is a moment to honor the passing cortege, blindly living
among the waking dead. the heart endures for now.

the song rises even in this quiet moment, audible for those
with ears to hear it, chant the unbidden dream.

Alvin Ailey's Ode

A flower in the field of blooms in black, laid
on the woman fallen below, stretched out still

innocent despite violence. the mourners come,
young women leaning to grieve, reaching out

gently to touch, to remember, to help her
rise again, gently to join the dance again, swing

become a celebration of her life, their loves,
a "morn by men unseen" full of grace, until

finally they must let her go, laying her down
to lie where she lay, and they mourners again:

thus we wade in the water, we rocka our souls,
we, risen to join the chorus, become dancers

in the great shared finale, O then rocka our souls
in the bosom of Abraham, O rocka our souls.

Chicago Springtime

Beyond coronavirus & Grant Park's shouting
politicians, the streets of Edgewater, lakeshore paths

fill with bicycles, gardeners in short sleeves clearing
plots & doorway pots, dogs prance on school lawns,

free spirits leaping in a new day sunshine, their people
swooning like lovers, couples hand holding in dreams

where later full moon twilight flashes down the alleys,
kids play pickup basketball dashing among trash cans,

wild after a winter of sighing at frost-etched windows,
surely as the poet muses in a common room window

above, sitting before a photo of Picasso, Eluard, Lacan,
a whole crowd of artists & poets, freed to share breath

on the Paris day of liberation, this moment come
unbidden—& finally, stillness, the midnight moon.

Silent March Candlelight Vigil for George Floyd

The march was to be silent meditation
from Rosa Parks Circle past the cop station
to the park candlelight vigil memory for
George Floyd—never got to candles nor light—
downtown erupted cars aflame, windows smashed,
the Vault of Midnight looted, Cuban Sanchez
Restaurant, Public Library, Art Museum windows
shattered—so many of these rioters were
laughing white boys—too much like Boogaloo Bois
or the agents provocateurs inciting violence,
cursing cops and bystanders in Ann Arbor or Detroit
late 60s—proved when Allen Ginsberg sat with me
over FOIA papers showing FBI connections then.
Ah, charnel house we live in, pandemic deaths riots
rebellions across the nation, leaders threatened by
thugs with assault rifles, a president's threats and lies.
What angels hover over us now? Which ghost riders
fill our evening skies? What dreams flee this night?
Ah, George Floyd, peaceful spirit, be with us now.

Love in the Corona

Turn off the news, hysteria rabid in tales vapid as
politicians' chortling rage and lies. where does
one find love in this sunrise with its promise?
Stillness over meadow & in budding willows,
crocuses still thrust in the cool air, the garden
strewn with clusters of daffodils, irises, snowdrops
not to be denied after the second death of winter—

Beyond, schools, restaurants, bars all shut down,
quaking clerks, silent shoppers wander grocery aisles,
ghosts groping for corn flakes, apples, oranges,
steaks & bacon, eyeing each other distantly, side-
stepping to avoid contact, this common humanity
in this newly waking alien world, groping for ways
to keep love safe, alive, sharing it with those losing it—

strange tongue in these flaming hours, relearning
the speech of love, now hopeful, tentative, full of loss
yet reaching through aether, hands & lips & eyes
seeking clarity if only in fleeting shared kindness.
Ah sunset's wild colors, deep shadows, new stars
suddenly here, and we, holding hands, fifty years
after the casual proposal—Ides of March.

January 6 Suite

Out of the Shadow

After lies more lies bullying walling out refugees
cutting treaties accords insulting allies mimicking
tyrants ripping children from their parents' arms,

black men & women strangled & shot by police,
marching goons the pose with a bible never read,
after so many dead on ventilators, choking apart

from their families while they die, the toll now rising
past a quarter million gone forever in memory
& sorrow—after lockdowns & alienation across

the land, militias threatening elected officials,
the human touch kind eyes & hearts lost, one
wonders how we all survived to see this day.

Yearning for Guan Yin's poured waters, for
mercy & quiet compassion, I too have failed.

Day of Liberation

Dancing! dancing in the street! Philadelphia PA,
city of brotherly love, shrine of continental congress,
framer of the Constitution delivered us, now

now resurrected for the new day, dancing with
abandon, set free at last. Here in the dooryard,
Bradford pear's autumn leaves glow like a torch

in the sunrise, this sign raised for the tired and poor,
those too sick to sing, the immigrant child caged
 in squalor separated from her family, black women

and DACA kids raising their eyes: when new night
unfolds, twilight now a mystery, it is a night for
dreams at last, for turning in a half-moon swathed

in stars, bathed in mist where the lovers float in
a sea of silence soaring toward dreams and daybreak:
new light, the shore where clear life may begin again.

Let all storms bring healing rain

Spurious lawsuits hearsay lies
Giuliani Sejanus to his Tiberius
all tossed as trash,

Supreme Court's curt denial,
armed thugs, senator stools spineless
suckers howling across the nation,

confederate threats, gnashing teeth—
the way will be torturous in spite
aimed at all hope, yet

Whitmer Benson & Nessel
all call for compassion & grace
facing down death threats.

Now, vaccines leave Portage,
Biden & Harris will be certified,
the long saga will begin,

in memoriam 300,000 now dead,
massive grief memorialized,
their love kept safe as memory:

Silence in the sunny room,
let all storms bring healing rain.

A Day

that shall live in infamy
smashed windows

senators representatives
in hiding, bullets thru doors,

offices ransacked bestial traitors
five dead, a nation shaken

all perpetrated by the worst
president in US history—

thanks to legislators
burning late night oil

standing signing new president
elected amid the loser's horrors.

hallelujah, O better angels
stay by us now.

Stillness, Silence

of the land January morning
white pine lateral branches

frenzy of witch hazel yellow flowers
red twig dogwoods above the snow

holly, young kousa straight & true
cedar with its nest of cardinals

river birch peeling bark & now
flicker at the suet feeder, crazy fat

squirrel upside down on hanging
seed cake, my 73rd birthday.

Onward, as Creeley used to sign

These gathering
hours decades screams & ecstasies,
testaments of open-eyed friends & lovers
the many passages that each
heart brings, contemplation
lost to kali yuga beyond—

pleasure, treasure
best minds of my generation,
beat outriders who came before us,
burgeoning younger voices
who will sing the days
we'll never see—

Silent serenity
thru storms, stars & huge wolf moon,
let jagged memory, earned wisdom
sing here with abandon
lives lived fearlessly
simple & plain.

Until Love Is Equal

Until love is equal, lovers will sigh
in their midnight beds, sing blues
in 3 a.m. rain for the agonies of friends
in pain, eyes weeping behind blind

windows, hands reaching for
a vanishing dream—sorrow
n the shattered lives and hearts,
in the fists of those too self-righteous
to know the brotherhood,

sisterhood of love. O naked
glad day boy in shining morning,
wake them all, O sisters in different
dawn, teach lack-love the love that heals,
the heart that may finally be free, the dance

that brings us all to our common breath,
lost loves' springtime pretty ringtime ayre.

Passing Phantoms

As the mission to Mars approaches landing
I walk out to my greenhouse in moonlight,
stars scattered across the sky in subzero cold,

recalling all those faces in the past year,
endless parade of sorrows and anxieties,
those headed west into sunset and deep night,

finding their way to the campfires of elders
bearing their dreams in medicine pouches
out among the music of spheres, dancing.

I dream youthful pleasures sail skating by night,
shoveling snow 4 a.m. predawn clearing
600 ft. driveway, alone in blue-lit forest silence,

ice shining on the river beyond, my waking
dream journey so my mother might drive out
at seven, cross town even on tortured sliding days,

dedicated to her students. I'd stride home
in silent forest's blue light, full moon thru branches—

eyes on the river's frozen dream and journey
to sunset and night, passing phantoms, as now.

Hour of the Ghost Dance

No more will the scioto madtom
swim in Ohio's Big Darby Creek,

gone are the ivory-billed woodpecker,
Backman's warbler never to sing again,

gone three species of pearly mussels,
the flat pigtoe mussel, southern acornshell,

stirrupshell lost among the 36 mussels &
70 freshwater snails gone, gone forever,

bridled white-eye, Little Mariana fruit bat,
San Marcos gambusia, plants they pollinate,

plants they reseed, all lost, lost forever, all
thru heavy hands crown-of-creation madness,

the age now a time of fleeting souls never
to return, superstorms raking coasts, drought

borne of Hetch-Hetchy presumptions, fires
leaping over mountains, ancient sequoias

licked by flames, volcanoes spitting fire,
thousands dead weekly—ghost dance hours,

sunset hours, time of the fleeting stars
whirling in ever-turning ever-burning sky.

Ukraine

Ah, Ukraine —years roll in a dead march, Saul killing thousands,
David tens of thousands, Arjuna the killer spurred by Krishna—

endless wars in China—Chen Zi'ang walking among shattered
bones, Du Fu hidden in his hut, lamenting horrors he witnessed,

fleeing never to return—a hundred years of killing celebrated
after Agincourt, then rockets red glare, bombs bursting in air,

Moscow shattered, Waterloo—Sumter Gettysburg Atlanta's flames
Richmond in ruins Sheridan amuck in Shenandoah, Sand Creek,

Tongue River, Wounded Knee, Custer—Ypres, Verdun, the Somme,
the Blitz, Dresden—the first death, the child in London. what stirs

such men—Hitler, Mussolini, Tojo, Stalin, now Putin the KGB thug
become manic nation butcher? what rage boils in their dreams that

they could act as now, in the European sunflower bread basket
forcing a good man to defiance, his peoples' heroism, cities

bombed to silence, refugees in millions fleeing nightmares,
what history, what twisted psyches in our human condition, what

ecce homo shatters lives, bodies, peace, kindness, compassion?
right after night I follow the moon walking the sky shining,

wondering at such tranquility, such silence, such a gift, tossed
for nightmares endless as hell's dark road, the agony of millions.

Thus spoke the old man, hoping to spend his last years in peace,
head in hands, sleepless nights with this hellish repetition—again.

Coda

Blessing for Volodymyr Zelenskyy, his wife Olena, their children,
Blessing for the wives and children living their nightmares,
  trapped on a long & dangerous road, even
  crossing borders to safety fraught with pain,
Blessing for the fathers, husbands and brothers forced to shoulder
  rifles, rocket launchers, Molotov cocktails,
  tearful by night and in quiet moments,
wondering if they'll live to see their loved ones again, if indeed
  those they love are safe.
Blessing for my poet friend Svitlana Iukhymovych, who translated
  the great dissident poet Vasyl Stus, dead in a Soviet
  prison 1985, still celebrated for his great courage today.
Blessing on the ruined cities of Ukraine, that they might live again,
Blessing on the Odessa Opera and Ballet Theatre, the long history
  of cultural excellence throughout Ukraine.
Blessing on the memory of Anna Akhmatova, born in Odessa
  recalled now as Anna of all the Russias,
Blessing on her poems, that they continue to speak truth to tyrants,
  that they liberate the minds & hearts of all who
  open her leaves, she shining star of world poetry.
Blessing on all nations who take in the refugees, feed & help them
  find lives beyond despair, may their families be reunited.
Blessing on those praying for the nation, the people, the children,
  that their dreams bear fruit & touch those in need.
May Ukraine rise from the ashes, free, & celebrate liberation
  & renewal, may the nation know liberty at last,
   celebrating survival in wild whirling
    dance & song.

Sanctuary

choose a large pot & fill it with good earth,
dig out holes for three tiny chrysanthemums—
too small, too late for planting out in garden—

free them from plastic pots and spread roots
so they can reach out into the soil, insulated now
under plastic wrap dome in the greenhouse,

ready now for coming winter's cold—a seedling
heating mat below them, there to be plugged in
when cold's too extreme. Outside, the sky changes

minute by minute, clouds & winds roaring
overhead, & in this darkness of hemlock
 & cedar leaves, rhododendron, oak & gingko,

there is still a silence where one may sing
& float a poem downriver, the full moon rising
in the blue wind. I lean where root meets stone

& sing a forlorn hope: these three may live to
stretch & grow in earth, flower in the new dawn.

Birthday Dreams for Andy

Andy, I look over your volumes in my sunny bedroom—
finest visionary poet of our time, true successor to the Beats,
wild basso profundo with fierce command of rhythm & sound
over years and decades, aware too of your strength as a man—

my first taste of your work *Shoe Be Do Be Ee-Op*,
its derelict women poets to come, the times *not* changing,
sea sick man on sidewalk asking for the star, *Festival of Squares*
tribute to the great workingman poet Jack Micheline,

visionary *Bo Baba* Put Yourself in this Body and then
We'll See How You Handle It Vacana, earlier birth of Ramona,
The Night Kerouac Died, Home of the Blues, Gokyo Lake
Breaking Up in the Sun, Shivaratri Time in Old Hardwar—

chronicling latter days of the Beat Generation, the years
from the Boulder Bandshell, NYC with Antler, driving
cross-country post-back surgery to Detroit, in Jersey City
barely able to stand yet delivering a powerhouse reading at

the Fox and Crow, all thankful you could join us. I think too
of your long search for love, finding it in the visionary romance
with Pamela. now, your struggle with foot and leg—always
the toughest of us, the best of us—may you rise above

this loss too, sing & shout true again—from Belgium, Oakland,
the many places touched by your presence, always a poet warrior,
deep well of inner strength, hod carrier poet, blues shouter,
great heart & powerful voice for the survival of love.

Spirit Walk Sunset

many nights flaming
sunsets over the great lake,
so many pause,
surrounded by lovers kith and kind—

desperate longings,
exhausted thought,
torrid clouds over waves,
silence on the horizon,
blues yellows scarlet flash
across the heavens,

purple cumulonimbus
all borne of western wildfires,
burned forests and homes, terror,
the dead and delirious.

Here, endless funerals, horrors,
a bride giving covid
to a young mother in reception line,
a dear friend's uncle dead,
family quarantined, one in the ICU—

after so many, one wonders indeed that
each is a first death unlike another.

this day is a quiet mass for one who gave all
to open paths for others, for their own lives,

sorrow rimmed in the eyes of survivors
yet welcoming to old friends, relatives,

and a long ride home melancholy reflection among
woods' mottled shade, long dry fields blueberry farms:

on a rare cloudless day dreaming of spirit walk sunset.
where will we be in a year, a decade, in memory?

Notes: Context of each book and notes to individual poems

Moonlight Rose in Blue follows Walt Whitman's editing practice for the 1891 deathbed edition of his work, retaining and revising poems he valued most from his eight previous editions of *Leaves of Grass*. I have selected work from each of my nine previous books, organizing each section as a movement in a collage of each time period I lived through. The notes for each section form an initial paragraph contextualizing the individual poems in their purview. This is the final and definitive version of the poems and has my approval as such.

DC 28 April 2025

The Rain: Early Poems 1970-1983

Most of these poems fit into the time frame of my first book, *Quiet Lives*. During this period, I had dropped out of college barely short of graduation, was newly married, struggling with my rage at the direction my nation had taken, horrified by the Vietnam conflict, the offhand violence of politicians in city streets across the nation. I was also discovering the lives of ordinary working people in factories, schools and restoration jobs for slumlords. These experiences were a revelation after years in academia, giving me a place among lives that had been very different from my own.

3   **Refugees.** First place, Kent County poetry awards adult category, 1971. Response to refugees fleeing their homes and livelihoods in Vietnam and elsewhere. Early effort scoring a poem for oral recitation derivative of William Carlos Williams per the letter to Richard Eberhart, 23 May 1954 in *The Selected Letters of William Carlos Williams* (pages 325-327), and "For Eleanor and Bill Monahan" as an example of this practice.

4   **American Dream: The Fall of Saigon.** It could be argued that much realist objectivist verse is mere reportage, yet these TV

images of the fall of Saigon were so striking, so *important*, that as I recorded them, any interpretive lines would not merely be superfluous, but would detract from the horror and tragedy of the fall.

5   **Lamentations.** A register of my disgust with the nation, voiced as surreal response to endless news of body counts of 200 or more boys my age each week, inability to be heard above the din of "politics as usual."

6   **Reliving the news.** Initial reaction to death of childhood friend Chris Clay, machine-gunned to death on his first recon mission in the demilitarized zone.

9   **The Rain.** Elegy for poet Charles Reznikoff (1894-1976) written after Allen Ginsberg let me know he had died. "Rezi" was one of those signal poets whose work was deeply important to my work as a writer. This poem was lost among two "early poems" manuscripts, rediscovered a few years back. I revised the third stanza for precision and published it in *Big Scream* 56 (2017). See *The Correspondence of David Cope & Allen Ginsberg 1976-1996*, pages 16 and 152, the latter for the many references to Charles in the first four decades of my career.

10   **The Exchange.** Visit to the New York Stock Exchange, early 70s.

11   **Operating Instructions.** In the summer before my 1970 marriage to Suzanne, I lived with my father to get to know him after 11 years of estrangement. I worked at Johnson Mold during that period, operating EDM machines that drilled holes in parts for airplane cooling systems. These instructions were accurate for a task that could be monotonous, though getting to know my former workers was an education after years in academia.

12   **Monday Morning.** Downtown street scenes in Grand Rapids. An early favorite poem.

13   **On the Road.** Madhouse traffic in Northern New Jersey, headed to Asbury Park with poet Bob Rixon, 1982. A visit to see Madame Marie's and The Stone Pony, but also to walk the boardwalk and enjoy Italian ices in midsummer. Later, we got caught in another traffic jam; the highlight of this part of the trip was the young drunks lifting their glasses to us all as a madhouse blessing.

14   **Paterson Falls.** A poem from the same visit as "On the Road," this is an homage to William Carlos Williams' epic poem, *Paterson*. "Williams' ball players"—a strange coincidence, finding a ball game being played in the park, immediately recalling the "minute figures" running on the diamond in Williams' *Paterson* (page 55). Locals: an immigrant family we met along the path, perfectly placed for inclusion in this poem. This work is slightly revised here, as I found it would work better in couplets.

15   **Roses.** An early love poem for Suzanne.

16   **Euclid Avenue.** Downtown street in Cleveland, a snapshot poem on the way to the Cleveland Museum of Art.

17   **Waiting for The Clash.** *Combat Rock* tour, appearance in Grand Rapids.

18   **Dreaming on You.** Elegy for my friend Todd and his older brother Don, killed in late night plane crash.

19   **7 a.m. Buffing the Floor.** Exterior doors locked until 8 a.m. at Hall School (now Cesar Chavez Academy), I buffed the hall floors after unlocking the interior doors. The neighborhood was beset with gangs and crime. This kid appeared at the door, wanted his

wounds dressed, but was suspicious of all authorities, perhaps covering his butt in the social pressures exerted by the gangs.

20   **Among Daisies & Lily Blossoms.** A study in personal loss shared by my neighbor, who rarely reached out to me, here needing to share his grief.

21   **Quitting Time.** Escape from factory hell.

22   **Train Crossing.** Hesitation at the crossing before going "yea-saying in the American night."

Quiet Lives (1975-1983)

I sent Allen Ginsberg a copy of my chapbook *Stars* in early 1976, and he wrote back, asking for 10 copies and sending me a check. Thus began a long and fruitful friendship, augmented by his awareness of my emerging vision and devotion to Charles Reznikoff. Allen helped me edit my work for a time, introducing me to Jim Cohn, who became my best friend and we opened ourselves to each other while working as first readers of each other's poems. Allen later wrote a note for me, hoping that his recommendation would give me openings for publication, also helping me win a Pushcart Prize and finding me a place in *New Directions Anthology #37* and *City Lights Journal #4*. Ultimately, I was invited to Naropa Institute, where I met my peers and gave lectures/recitations on Charles Reznikoff and Marsden Hartley. These years involved intense learning about my chosen career, editing of the manuscript of this first book and furious composition of new poems. The original manuscript was 156 pages, and I cut over 100 of these as not my best work, then composed the latter portion of the book to bring it to 88 pages. Tom Lanigan at Humana Press wanted the book, and so my voyage began.

25   **American Dream.** 1974 police shootout with the "Symbionese Liberation Army," a left-wing group who refused to surrender and burned to death when their house caught fire.

26   **Abandoned Hotel.** Search for furniture with a friend, weekend work to supplement my income from my factory job.

27   **A Quiet Life.** The Pham family (Tham and Lien, 6 kids) Sue and I sponsored for immigration and resettlement in US. Here, Vietnamese adults explain why other family members can't come to US now, Lien explaining the seasonal and pirate dangers of the journey.

28   **The Welfare Office.** The case worker reads: "drove buses Saigon to Hanoi 2 years," Tham's work back in his homeland, a ticket to a job in US "once he learns English."

29   **Tears.** Crying woman on a bench near cemetery atop Hall St. hill. She reminded me of Picasso's "Weeping Woman," in both cases the visual sorrow a tragic mystery writ large.

30   **The Shotgun.** Tragic tale overheard at the Elite Diner, Division Street, Grand Rapids.

31-34   **Empty Street, End of the Shift, Paint Work, The Landlady.** Four poems from my factory and weekend work, the psychology of poverty on display.

35   **The Plumber.** Lunch break in front of custodial office, Hall School, Grand Rapids. "Kraut," derogatory reference to German soldier.

36-37   **Peace.** A poem in two sections. 1. Breakroom Blues: 1975, custodial breakroom at Lincoln School for students with special needs. Some of my fellow custodians were Vietnam veterans still processing horrendous memories. As early as 1970, I *knew* that I would have to write this poem, but I had to hear memories of those years from Vietnam vets up close, as well as to develop my skills as a poet to write it later. 2. Ann Arbor: 1970, student antiwar protests, beatings by police, my senior year at U of Michigan—I dropped out to marry and seek a different way, only my poetry staying with me at that time—these two sections displaying the still-unhealed breach in my generation.

38 **A View from the Road.** Veteran's Hospital and Grounds, viewed from I-96. Grand Rapids, Mi.

39 **A Million Mute Corpses Speak.** Alexander Haig, claiming he's "in control" before the Senate.

40 **Burning Babies.** Conflict breaking off talks between Begin (Israel) and Sadat (Egypt), with tragic consequences.

41 **The Odor of Death.** Set in Nicaragua and adapted from news, Somoza's planes strafe refugees.

42 **Slagboom Tool & Die.** Tham's attempt to get a job; I accompanied him as his English was difficult for interviewers. Those who had jobs displayed their racism openly.

43 **CETA Office.** With the Pham family. The clerk's suggestion that there might be a job for Tham. CETA: Comprehensive Employment and Training Act, passed in 1973.

44 **Crash.** My most published poem, notably as a Pushcart Prize winner (1977), in *New Directions 37* (1978) and in the Beacon Press Anthology, *Poems to Live By in Troubling Times* (2006). Seen on US 16, Cascade Road.

45 **Lunch Hour.** Craps game among laid-off workers outside my custodial office window, Hall School (now Cesar Chavez Academy).

46 **Turning.** A poem responding to a local publisher's request for a poem on nuclear war. Not difficult to write, as my generation grew

up with continuous threat of nuclear attack, central to the Cold War.

48   **Chinese Calligraphy.** T'ang Yin, Freer Gallery, the only place in Washington, D. C. where I could in any way feel at ease.

49   **Rexroth Gone.** Spanish dead, Sacco & Vanzetti, Dylan Thomas: subjects of Rexroth's poems. My elegy and homage to him.

50   **Baseball.** Ball diamond with lights on the Thornapple River, Ada, Mi.

51   **Labor Day.** Republished in *Visiting Walt: poems inspired by the life and work of Walt Whitman.* Iowa U P, 2003.

52   **The First Death.** A second elegy for my childhood friend Chris Clay (see page 6 for the first). "The First Death": allusion to Dylan Thomas's famed line, "after the first death, there is no other," the final line in "A Refusal to Mourn the Death, by Fire, of a Child in London."

54   **Sweeping.** Quaker work ethic with a wink.

On the Bridge 1983-1986

My second book received the 1988 Academy and Institute of Arts & Letters Award (now American Academy of Arts & Letters), selected by Allen Ginsberg, James Dickey, and Irving Howe. *On the Bridge* came rapidly; I was sure of my subjects, experimented more with a variety of classic techniques, the use of metrical feet to perfect lines for oral recitation, greater compression of images, still keeping focus on ordinary subject matter: custodial work, apartment cleanup, people in their neighborhoods, camping, canoeing, war, wounds & PTSD. Grand Rapids, Hoboken & NYC.

57   **Party Talk.** A high school friend's changed attitude after returning from Vietnam, with my memory of another sending a "gift" from the front.

59   **Antietam.** Sue's father's PTSD after killing a German officer face-to-face in World War II, juxtaposed with three parts of the Antietam battlefield, the horror of the losses in a landscape of great beauty. Antietam: battle in the Civil War, largest loss of life in a single day—23,000 killed, wounded and missing. 17 September, 1862.

60   **The Liberty Bell.** Crowd responses to this American symbol.

61   **CIA Manual Discovered.** Online: see CIA Assassination Manual 1950s.

62   **Alone.** weekend work for slumlord.

63   **Blue April.** "tu-tones"—two-toned shoes, often brown and beige or black and white.

64   **At the Croyden.** Weekend work, as above. This poem is a companion to "The Invisible Keys" (pages 90-91).

65   **Old Woman in the Café Window.** First poem written after transfer from Hall Elementary School to Grand Rapids Junior College, a move from an ethnic neighborhood to fast-paced downtown business district.

66   **"Take Care of Yourself."** Gesture by an old man in Bryant Park, NYC, when Jim Cohn and I stopped to see poet James Ruggia at his bookstall job, en route to Allen Ginsberg's apartment and my later reading and impromptu book launch of *Quiet Lives*. 67th Street YMCA, 15 March 1983.

67   **Landlady on the Stoop.** Willow Avenue, Hoboken, N. J.

68   **The Breakwater.** A childhood memory of fishing with my father after his and my mother's divorce, on the Muskegon breakwater.

69   **Further Progress.** A poem for poet Nate Butler, shot in the head by a junkie intent on robbing poets giving a reading at Gaia Coffee House.

70   **The Old Stebbens Place.** Ruined farmhouse in woods near Pines Point campground on the White River, Manistee National Forest near Hesperia, Mi.

71   **Taylor Bridge to Pines Point.** Companion poem to "The Old Stebbens Place."

72   **Sears Service Center Waiting Room.** Watching the funeral of India's prime minister Indira Gandhi while waiting for my car to be repaired, among restless customers.

73   **Midwinter Cleanup.** Tale told by World War II veteran/co-worker during winter school cleanup at Dickinson Elementary School, Grand Rapids.

74   **New Windows.** House on Jefferson Street not far from Burton, my labors eased by women on the floor above singing with gusto. Grand Rapids, Mi.

75   **Getting the Pump Out.** Collaborative labors, G-1 receiving room, GRCC.

76   **The Flood.** Spring floods on the Owashtanong (Grand) River near Johnson Park, Walker, Mi.

77   **Mottled Wings.** The hawk soaring above the canoeists on Big Manistee River,—the graceful flight of one bird, while others see their own loss in it.

78   **Easter.** A young girl's gesture of recognition with a tired workman kept away from his own family by the need for money to pay their bills.

79   **Rhubarb.** Gesture between Joe Hale and me as his wife (Sue's grandmother) lay dying in her bed, attended by women relatives.

81   **My Father.** A memory of visiting my father's workplace, Dilesco, in Muskegon, Mi. with his defense of my poems to my Aunt Frances, who thought them useless for income.

82   **The Lights of St. Ignace.** The first of my free sonnets, written in a tent in the wilderness outside St. Ignace, Mi. I was reading Ted Berrigan's sonnets at the time.

83   **On the Main Road.** The first of a suite of four work poems, featuring a predawn tanker accident on I-196, the flare of the flames lighting up the scene, police and ambulance racing out of the city, all this seen from Chicago Drive, a road running parallel to the highway. I was on my way to work, opening 200 doors at the college where I worked, and on this morning, preoccupied with the fate of the driver, learning later that he lived.

84   **Memorial Stone.** Visit to Veterans Park, tracing names of friends killed in Nam, recalling their lives and predilections—one of the winos in the park, seeing my sorrow, offered me a slug of wine.

85   **Soft Rain.** Short line couplets, observing a family enjoying their time together on the porch.

86   **Moonlight & Sunrise.** Published in University of Michigan *LSA* magazine.

Fragments from the Stars 1986-1990

This is the last of my books written during my blue collar years; through much of that time, I was a head custodian at GRCC, but was hired to teach freshman English in 1987—blue collar by day, professional white collar in evenings. This change was perhaps spurred by awards and publication, as well as my teaching at Naropa Institute summer sessions. *Fragments* follows the births of my second and third children, the wounds suffered by workers on their jobs, the desperation of job loss and recession, environmental decay, the agony of war, Tiananmen Square massacre, loss of friends. These poems highlight my life in a time of transition even as I maintained the real work—my poetry—true to my expanding vision.

89   **Industrial Clinic.** Clinic on or near 6th Street, Grand Rapids, where working folk were attended to by company doctors— treatment sometimes a kind of crucifixion.

90   **The Invisible Keys.** Companion poem to "At the Croyden" (page 64). My first true blues poem, editing via metrical changes to underline emotive turns in the poem. The poem also makes use of a Berrigan-like list in the first section, deploying off-balance line breaks to mimic the rising action of the music, moving off-margin lines in the manner of Williams to record the crowd's internal feelings as the solo rises to crescendo.

93   **"Hot Coals Burning on Your Tongue."** Beginning in December, 1987, the first Intifada continued a pattern of conflict with Israel dating back decades, this time Palestinians forming Hamas. The poem records Israeli soldiers' violence against Palestinian civilians, turning to the young boy in tears, and his enraged older brother.

94   **Tiananmen Square Sequence.** Now known as the "June 4 incident" in China, where the subject is not to be spoken of. I recognized the significance of this event as it occurred and wrote the sections of this poem as it unfolded. The poem was originally cast as four separate poems, but I soon realized that the parts all belonged together, following the sequence of events while preserving the discrete quality of each part of the poem.

96   **Iran.** Iraqi poison gas attack on rural northern Iranian towns.

97   **On Ramp at Rush Hour.** Camaraderie of homeless folk observed from the window of a passing bus.

98   **Rainy Dawn.** A mentally stressed person among others waiting for a predawn bus, struggling to make sense of her confusion.

99   **The New Foot.** G-1 floor, Receiving, GRCC Main Building, honoring a co-worker who'd had his foot amputated.

100   **Alex Jane.** Birth of my second child, Alex Jane.

102   **New Moon.** Backyard of my home in Grandville three blocks from the rail line where the "bomb train"—loaded with dangerous industrial chemical wastes—comes by late at night from Dow Chemical of Midland, Mi.

104   **For Suzanne.** Early memento of falling in love. "Let's be famous lovers" is the dedicatory verse in "The Rhododendron" (page 171).

105   **Will.** Birth of my third child, Will. Poem was written on a hospital napkin near the bed where Sue was resting. One draft complete

106   **Albeniz, Sor & Sanz.** Commuters reward a classical guitarist in the subway even as they shun beggars at the turnstiles.

107   **Sleep.** I was teaching Walt Whitman's *Leaves of Grass* to my freshmen after my daughter Alex's birth, and this poem may have been influenced by a class reading of "The Sleepers," albeit on a much smaller scale. Sleep" begins with my visit to Alex's room when she was sleeping, tender moment both in the beginning and later in the final verse paragraph, which rounds out a brief catalog of folk whose sleep is restorative in their various situations. This poem in no way attempts the expansive verse made by father Whitman, other than as a small form exploration of the rest accorded to all who sleep and dream.

108   **Old Man.** An aged derelict lying against a subway wall, one of many without hope.

109   **Killings to be Made in Soybean Futures.** As the news advises investors to put their funds in soybean futures, an oldtimer laments the end of his career even as others learn the double meaning of killings.

110   **For Billy.** A poem for old friend Billy Breidenfield, dying of ALS. He had asked me to write a prayer for him.

111   **Before I Leave for the Mountains.** Aware that Billy's health was dramatically deteriorating, I stopped over at his house to help with his daily treatments, caring for him now as my only way to show him my love. I departed the following day to drive to Naropa in Boulder, Co., keeping him in mind as I recited my poems and taught the work of other poets to the students.

112   **Gone West.** Colloquial: gone to the ancestors in the afterlife. Tonto National Monument, Arizona.

113   **Chorus of Snores.** Cabin bunkhouse at Phantom Ranch, on the floor of the Grand Canyon. Snoring men, unconscious masculine selves revealed in their snoring. Poem written on a rock in the lighted path to Anasazi ruins near the Colorado River.

114   **Diné Woman.** Companion poem to "Chorus of Snores," this poem is a portrait of a Diné (Navaho) woman selling her wares to white tourists along the road in the reservation.

115   **July.** Portrait of my daughter Anne at 14, her future opening before her.

116   **Harvest Sundown.** Elegy for Scott MacIntyre, brother to my best friend in high school, Todd (see page 18). Scott was a champion polo player, and in later years, a ranch hand out west.

118   **Sundown.** A quiet chant, evening epiphany..

119   **After the Long Hard Day.** A poem for my beloved.

Coming Home 1990-1993

Thomas Lanigan writes that *Coming Home* "binds together two major strands of Cope's life and art. . . both the clear-eyed strider of our broken cities [and] the profoundly lyrical explorer of nature, of redemptive human nature in all its silence and nakedness." This book contains my final custodial poems and is the first in the second half of my working years, now a post-graduate student and college professor studying Shakespeare and his contemporaries, Dante, Chaucer, Old English, and Norse Literature, yet it is predominantly shadowed by environmental degradation, the Gulf War and the horrors that have flowed from these ever since.

123   **The Return.** Dreamed spirit journey, encompassing millenia.

124   **Armstrong to Gothics.** Mountains in the Adirondacks, upstate New York. These stanzas were written as the Allies geared up for the Gulf War: at once four discrete poems or one four stanza

poem. I read my poems at St. Lawrence University, and afterwards, Jim Cohn and I did this two day hike in the Adirondacks together.

126   **Coming Home.** Vers libre tercets modeled on the compression (if not the exact form) in Dante's *Commedia*. The certainty of the coming war in the departure of young soldiers, only Sue waiting in the doorway as I come home makes this bearable.

127   **Fireball in the Clouds.** First days of the Gulf War, January, 1990. Return of the surreal.

129   **In Fitful Sleep.** Reawakening in the nightmares of war.

130   **Below the Headlines.** Vice President Cheney and Chairman of the Joint Chief of Staff Powell making light of allies' progress in the Gulf War, as the poem moves to explore the horrors of the conflict.

131   **The Front Lines.** Iraqi Republican Guard trapped on front lines.

132   **Ghazal for the Coming Spring.** "shamal": northwesterly wind and blinding sandstorms blowing across the Gulf region in summer.

133   **Words.** The effects of political lies given credence in the media.

134   **Sunday Morning.** Weekend building check, a perk for head custodians, ensuring that all is secure.

135   **Pointing It Up.** A poem written while watching a workman seven stories up, viewed out my classroom window as students and I worked on writing samples—this being my effort.

136 **AP Wire Story: "Janitors at Risk."** A favorite poem, as it catches key notes from my work experience, ending with a blessing from childhood memory.

137 **The Abandoned.** At this stage of my life, I rode the bus to work through ramshackle neighborhoods, here observing a family playing in their world.

138 **Pacific Sundown.** Malibu beachfront.

139 **Sierra Madre & North to Oregon.** Pollution on beaches and mountains, humans destroying the planet.

140 **Audubon in Fog: The Descent.** Spiritual practice in descent.

142 **A March Blessing.** Bringing my son Will down to the Owashtanong (Grand) River to see the springtime flood for the first time, musing too on the flooded skulls of those buried in the thousand year old Hopewell Mounds, remembering lost friends racing naked with me on dark paths. The poem ends with lessons for Will.

143 **Catching Nothing.** "Anne"—my eldest child. Stanza 3: "you"— my paternal grandmother, Helen Cope. "Wiltshire to Delaware"— my ancestors emigrated from Wiltshire, England to Naiman's Creek, Delaware in 1680, eventually settling in Bradford, Pa. The "dinosaur bone collector" is the most famed of my ancestors, the 19th century paleontologist and herpetologist, Edward Drinker Cope. Marquette: French Jesuit missionary and explorer, who traveled throughout the Great Lakes. Poem is a meditation on the beauty of the storm while camping at Pines Point wilderness, near the same route that Father Marquette took on his last trip, dying near Ludington and dug up later to be buried in St. Ignace near the present-day Ojibwe Museum.

146   **For Helen Cope.** Elegy for my paternal grandmother—my grandfather's second wife.

147   **Midsummer Night.** "sea of sadness": samsara, per Buddhist belief. Yet this is a time for love.

148   **The Abandoned City.** An apocalyptic civilization-ending nightmare.

149   **Convent Garden.** Summer school for local Anishinaabe people, then situated in the former Carmelite monastery on the West side of Grand Rapids. "Migwetch": giving thanks in the language of First People living in Michigan and nearby states.

150   **For Fin & George.** Elegy for young Finvola Drury, daughter of Fin and George, sibling of brother young George. Young Fin spent her adult years giving compassionate care to AIDs patients, yet her death was unrelated to her work. This poem later appeared on the AIDs quilt, which was displayed in many cities nationwide.

151   **Farewell.** An elegy of conscious hyperbole for my friend Billy Breidenfield.

152   **The River.** Elegy for Elva Van Haitsma, a professor at Grand Rapids Community College who often invited me to read and speak to her poetry students when I was still working as a custodian.

153   **White Light.** A poem for Allen Ginsberg, celebrating the love among poets after his reading and visit to GRCC. "Kinnickinnick": an Ojibwe word referring to red twig dogwood or bearberry mixed with tobacco and smoked.

154   **In Heavy Clouds, in Cold Rain.** Poem written on a bus after waiting at bus stop on Porter and Byron Center, Wyoming, Mi. Sympathy for a frantic fellow passenger.

155   **March.** A poem bending to the prevailing winds, whether in the natural world or in this current stage of life, the aging singer finding only paradox.

156   **For All Lost Love.** Two lovers who've lost their love, also a chant for all lost love. Tercets.

157   **"What Thou Lovest Well."** Title is from Exra Pound's Canto LXXXI, pages 520-522, from *The Cantos of Ezra Pound,* New Directions, sixth printing, 1977.

158   **Each Wound Became a Voodoo Mouth.** Poem responds to the acquitted officer in the Rodney King case and the riots that followed. "90210": a TV comedy featuring privileged white kids oblivious to issues beyond their partying. Poem finale turns to the horrors of slavery via slaves escaping from a sinking ship to the "alien shore" with "no common language but anger."

159   **El Mozote.** Poem on the massacre of 800-1200 people in El Mozote, El Salvador, perpetrated by a death squad trained by American military advisors. See Wikipedia: El Mozote massacre.

160   **Poem Beginning with a Line by Pound.** "The enormous tragedy of the dream in the peasant's bent soldiers" is the opening line of Pound's Canto LXXIV; I have quoted it as the key note in response to George H. W. Bush's State of the Union address in 1992.

161   **For the Old Man's Tears.** "the gateless gate": is from a book of koans, which according to A. V. Grimstone embodies "some element of zen teaching" to help the student in his training. See

Two Zen Classics" Mumonkan & Hekiganroku. Ed. Katsuki Sekida. WeatherHill, 1977. Pages 26-27.

162   **Ghost Dance for La Grande Vitesse.** A dream of midnight in the central plaza of the banking and government area of downtown Grand Rapids, the sterility of values implicit in the steel and glass buildings surrounding Alexander Calder's bright red stabile, *La Grande Vitesse.* The dream also includes the first people of the area, now shades moving silently among those who visit the plaza for an annual art festival celebration. I celebrate the Calder, the one transcendent part of this plaza, as well as noting the native presence from a time when the banks of the Owashtanong River were theirs for their communities, lives and fishing in a more spiritually aware way of life.

165   **A Prophecy.** Poem explores the paradigm shift announced by the current generation of futurists, whose rosy predictions of a future renaissance ignore the disasters of the past.

166   **The Lovers Sleep.** The caged shaman is Leonard Peltier, Lakota activist imprisoned for murder on scant evidence. The "unruly master" is from a line in William Carlos Williams's "For Eleanor & Bill Monahan," a favorite poem of mine.

167   **Satie & Dante.** "the silences between syllables" or notes is the signal motif of both Satie's Music and Williams's "variable foot," but it is also a keynote of Dante pilgrim's journey through Paradise, where listening and learning are prerequisites for spiritual enlightenment.

168   **A Charm.** A charm in the Old English mode, perhaps borne of William Blake's early poems in their imagery.

Silences for Love 1993-1998

Silences continues the exploration of middle age and its vicissitudes, but is also a coming home to my Michigan and its inland seas. The elegy for Allen Ginsberg, "for allen," is a key poem here, a point at which I had to redefine my own priorities, giving up pursuit of PhD after 7 straight years of racking up 4.0 g.p.a. while teaching up to 19 hours of classes, continuous editing and publication of my books and *Big Scream* magazine, and raising my family. This book explores the need for silence to find some personal space beyond the noise of the world.

171   **The Rhododendron.** My "signature" poem, performed at almost every reading. Quote for Suzy is from "For Suzanne," a memory of our days of falling in love in Ann Arbor, 1970 (page 104). Poem celebrates the springtime beauty of the rhododendron in bloom, but it's also a meditation on enduring love, shared memories and the inability to define what love is other than through the paradox of eye, hand and heart, turning to other memories—teardrop on a granite peak in the Rockies, kids playing "midnight ghost" around the big oaks in my childhood woods near the Thornapple River, turning at last to the opening lines, completing the circle.

172   **Alba: The Sailors.** "Alba": in the Provençal troubadour tradition is a farewell song between lovers parting at dawn.

173   **Two Women Dream Together.** Companion poem to "Alba: The Sailors."

174   **for allen.** Paean and farewell to my mentor, poet Allen Ginsberg. This elegy recalls 5 shared memories: Allen's farewell call in the night prepared me to compose it, the parts simply a matter of choosing which memories to recall. Composition involved following my mind's lead as I allowed it to clear, thus: 1. 1986, I came to Boulder to read in Andy Clausen's series; Allen invited me

to stay in the "mansion on the hill" owned by his college friend. Poet Chris Ide and I were given tasks such as watering plants in the garden and doing light housework, while Peter Orlovsky cooked a big pot of chicken soup. Chris and I got wild by day, racing around the house in our underwear, settling to read poems in the library, going to the evening readings and wandering around Boulder in the dark. 2. Visit to Allen's place in NYC to read with Eliot Katz and others in Brooklyn series, the time also memorable for films on Allen's little TV—Allen at the Wailing Wall, Jerusalem, and Charles Reznikoff, his reading intro'd by George Oppen. 3. Summer session in Boulder where Allen had injured his thigh while trying to restrain Peter Orlovsky, singing songs by Campion and Dowland in Allen's apartment with Steven Taylor. 4. A memory of Buddhist retreat near my home. 5. Meeting after his reading at Hill Auditorium, Ann Arbor with charge to extend the lineage. I wrote this after Bill Morgan called me in the morning, to let me know that Allen had passed and to ask if I would serve as a news contact fielding calls from journalists. Poem was written in one draft, no revisions.

176   **sirens & flashing lights stop.** Detroit newspaper strike, 1995. Divide-and-conquer tactics on owners' parts—lower wages attracting out-of-work laborers to subvert union workers against each other via paycheck.

177   **The Cranes.** Surreal images, apocalyptic mode.

178   **Two Hearted River.** This river flows north into Lake Superior, and is at least in name the setting for Ernest Hemingway's "Big Two-Hearted River." A "gunnel" is the gunwale, top edge of the side of a canoe or boat. "Paradise or Mackinac": town and city at the confluence of Lakes Michigan and Huron; "stormy Mondays" is a play on the title of the famed jazz song of the same name.

180 **He took a long pull on the stout, thanked us all.** As we camped near the Two Hearted River, a local from nearby Newberry showed up, angry at the dislocations caused by Governor John Engler's closing a hospital which cared for the disabled in the area in order to build a prison there—forcing families to go 300 miles south to care for their disabled members, and throwing folk out of work.

181 **In the Alley.** Satiric dispute between young and old.

182 **The Job.** Elegy for my co-worker and friend Benny, also featured in "Peace," pages 36-37. This poem was written after his early death,.

183 **Thru Gary & Calumet to the Monet.** Intense pollution and unemployment in northern Indiana. Picasso's "blue guitarist" is here a homeless man in Chicago.

184 **push off.** Spring canoeing trip on Big Manistee River (northern lower peninsula of Michigan.)

186 **Memory in Love.** Elegy for gifted younger poet, Chris Ide, who died of overdose in 1994. See "for allen" for shenanigans we shared earlier (page 174).

187 **Many Reunions.** Summer "Beats and Other Rebel Angels" conference, Naropa Institute (now University), Boulder, Co. 1994.

188 **New Life.** Among crowds of singing poets, a declaration of love for a dear friend.

189 **A Vision in Manistique.** City atop Lake Michigan, with memory of childhood trip on Milwaukee Clipper from Muskegon to Milwaukee and back.

190   **The Mirror of Heaven.** Kitch-iti-kipi Spring, Palms Book State Park, along US 2.

191   **leaving classes.** My own internal struggle, family snapshot, fears of cancer via years of misbehavior, finale in relief.

192   **the hidden meadow.** Pastoral visions while climbing along the Rocky Mountains' front range above Boulder.

194   **all night.** a husband's struggle, unable to relieve his wife's pain.

195   **For Martin King.** 15 line vers libre sonnet, paean to Dr. King written for annual MLK Day Celebration performed at Fountain Street Church, Grand Rapids, Mi. The "flesh made word" is an inversion of "the word made flesh" (John 1: 14) and "that bones may walk" is a paraphrase of Ezekial 37: 1-14.

196   **Turning.** Hiking to the store, aware of the presence of a spirit beside me, watching over me, aware too that I could be going mad —until a homeless man emerged from behind a dumpster, snapping me out of this reverie.

197   **no time to feel.** Driving south through Allegan County on US 131 in a snowstorm, suddenly spinning out of control, no time to feel my own death approaching me, then an apparent silence and need for quick awareness and action for survival.

198   **April.** Spring awakening.

199   **Free Clothes.** Distribution of clothes to those in need after the long winter. Another awakening.

Turn the Wheel 1998-2003

Turn the Wheel opens with a lean dawn, lost loves, past sorrows and tenderness filling the older poet's dreams, tender petals for calm crossing.

Here are ground zero struggle for compassion, lost worlds in the valley of the sun, finale a struggle for love in a broken world, a farewell to "weird sisters, spellweavers, politicians."

203   **Lost Loves.** Visitation by spirits of lost loves in the dark night, secret fires, Love that floods lost dreams.

204   **Fran.** My father's eldest sibling, a woman whose life was epic in its suffering and survival, in age the "wise woman" of our family.

206   **Solihull to Marylebone.** Train from Solihull to London from my 1999 visit to England, preparing me for teaching Shakespeare by seeing Royal Shakespeare Company and Globe Theatre productions of plays by Jonson and Shakespeare. This train trip allowed me to see the 400 year production of *Julius Caesar* with an all-male cast at the Globe, the play exploring the Roman civil war that led to tyranny. The poem also refers to sorties over Kosovo, a side trip to Coventry where I was shown downtown areas bombed by Nazis, leading to revenge bombing of Dresden in the second world war: the horrors of our own time strangely echoed in the play itself.

207   **Reading the Signs.** Wilderness hiking as spiritual practice.

208   **Ghazal of the High Plateau.** The "yellow flower, an unearthly flower" is from William Carlos Williams' "The Yellow Flower," employed here as allusion. The phrase "now blazoning Broadway": Broadway may have been a deer path before Europeans came to the continent. "The ayre" is a renaissance art song, such as those by composer-lutenists Campion, Dowland. I employ the middle-eastern ghazal form quite loosely here, as a series of long-lined couplets, each of which turns the subject in a different direction.

210   **Tender Petals for Calm Crossing.** A poem wishing Jim Cohn well on his South American trip. Thus "stone masons" built

Macchu Picchu in Peru. "Hungry ghosts" refer to spirits unable to let go of a past life, trapped in desire per Tibetan Kagyu belief. This poem is one of a trio of poems written as free-form ghazals, the other two being "Ghazal of the High Plateau" and "The dharma at last." I love this poem first because it's a good will gesture to Jim and second, what Pablo Neruda found when he passed through here, as seen in his famed *Alturas de Macchu Picchu*, third because its movement thru anaphorae with "here" as the base word for the chant ranges from what you will find and what you'll leave, as Pablo did.

212   **The dharma at last.** "boys leap": as children, we used to leap from a 30 foot cliff into the river where I grew up. The poem proceeds from the innocent opening image to a police lineup at the 1968 Democratic National Convention, but also to many protests for peace in Vietnam and against the co-option of the American democratic process. The "one-eyed bard" is an oblique reference to Allen Ginsberg, who led protesters away from the police riot in Grant Park at the Democratic Convention, but also to the Norse god Odin, who traded his eye to the Norns for wisdom. In his later years, Allen's eye was continually weeping, a condition caused by clogged ducts—a bit of a stretch to the one-eyed bard.

215   **In Silence.** A poem written for my cousin Dr. Ann Barber, who served in the Emergency ward at St. Vincent's Hospital, one of those hospitals put on 24 hour shifts after the 9-11 tragedy. The "Winter Garden, Palm Court" refers to a palm-lined portion of the atrium seen in photos after the tragedy (not the Palm Court of the uptown Plaza Hotel). Photos sent to me by poet James Ruggia– source for these lines..

216   **Blue Notes for New York.** Twin Towers disaster, paean and lament for the nation's greatest city.

217   **Ground Zero.** A poem set on the stairs of the North tower of the North Building at Grand Rapids Community College, written on 9-11. The sorrows of the two young women, the dark stranger and the rush hour crowds presented me with a strangely emblematic enigma on this day of national tragedy.

218   **Bomb Fragments, Body Parts.** The horrors borne of the complex history of Afghanistan and the Middle East, ordinary people on the goat paths of that region shown from above on TV, and the place of Western oil addiction in all of this.

219   **The Disappearing Sages.** Enlightenment philosopher Voltaire and Prospero, the "magus himself," disappear, their wisdom as vanity in a world where "the last standing man is Caliban" and even "the alchemy of the word" is given a farewell, only silence left to "heal the brainsick heart at last." The poem may be inspired by Salvador Dalí's "Slave Market with Disappearing Bust of Voltaire," though my poem has the wise man disappearing through flowers, not a slave market. The notion of the vanity of the wise is intact.

220   **The Gift.** Elegy for Billy Breidenfield, read at his funeral.

221   **Gone (as you are).** Kayaking on the Big Manistee River, Hodenpyl Dam to Red Bridge.

222   **Owashtanong Sunrise.** Remains of the rapids on the downtown stretch of the Owashtanong (Grand) River in the 1990s. The logjams are the *debacle* of 1883 which tore through downtown Grand Rapids, smashing bridges etc. The drama of the poem, however, involves an old fisherman's struggle to catch a "big one."

224   **The white bristled sallow face in the photo.** Homeless man found dead under freeway overpass near the route of my morning hikes along the river in the 1990s. Companion poem to "Owashtanong Sunrise," a study in contrast.

225   **After Ronsard.** Adaptation (not translation) from Pierre de Ronsard's Sonnet 26 in the second book of *Sonnets Pour Hélène*, with contemporary references from September 11, 2001.

226   **The Fourth.** A Muslim refugee couple struggling with their immigration to the U. S.

227   **In a Sentimental Mood.** A poem written to the sound of John Coltrane's "In a Sentimental Mood," with sorrow of one lover, his loss set against Manhattan's rush and history.

228   **Canyon Rim to Hopi Point Sunrise.** Predawn hike along South rim of the Grand Canyon, memory of lost loves. "Cardenas" refers to García López de Cárdenas y Figuroa, first European to see the Grand Canyon, August 1540. The "Anasazi & Havasupai" are first people nations native to the Canyon, Anasazi present now only in their ruins, while the Havasupai continue to live there, apart from tourist trails.

229   **Lear by Lanternlight.** Reading *King Lear* late at night in my tent along the Big Manistee River while my companions snored in their tents.

230   **Yeah, an' here he was.** Dream visit from the spirit of Allen Ginsberg, with a memento of my generation's poets met through Allen's good graces—and their struggle with that loss. "Dreams deferred" utilizes the famed line from Langston Hughes' poem, "What happens to a dream deferred?" implying my generation's need to pick up the work.

232   **"La Goulue" considers his lines.** Persona of the French can-can dancer, famous via Toulouse Lautrec's painting, adapted here to the middle-aged poet's dilemma, with a little gender-bending.

234   **Madadayo in Dreams.** *Madadayo* is Akira Kurosawa's last film.
wherein the revered professor meets annually with his former
students, who ask him if he is "ready" (to face death), his answer
being "madadayo" (not yet). The poem is a dream visit by lost
friends Allen Ginsberg and Chris Ide, the mode surreal. "Jimmy" is
Jim Cohn, my best friend. "Satie" is Erik Satie, whose piano works
are meditative in tenor. "The third thought not my death" refers to
Prospero's lines "and thence retire me to my Milan, where every
third thought shall be my grave" (*The Tempest*, Arden ed. 5.1.312).

236   **Out thru the eye beyond the stars.** A night sailing upriver on the
Thornapple River, coupled with desire to send the moonlight itself
to Jim Cohn, who had recently lost his mother.

The Night Blooming Cereus 2003-2007

The Night Blooming Cereus honors two of my singing fathers, Robert Hayden
and Carl Rakosi, though the dominant theme in this set involves poems
reacting to the Gulf War, especially the horrors of Abu Ghraib and
Haditha. "October Surprise" is a poem requested by Ed Sanders, re the
concern that Republicans would spring such a surprise on the nation just
before the election. The set turns away to other themes in its final poems.

239   **The Night Blooming Cereus.** Our night blooming Cereus, a gift
from the Breidenfield family after father Jack died, blooms several
times a year, each time for a single night of beauty and fragrance.
This poem celebrates the brief flowering, but also salutes my first
mentor, the great Robert Hayden, via his poem of the same name.

240   **Masks of Six Decades.** As I reached my sixth decade, I paused to
reflect on the many personae of the various illusions that got me
through the madness of each period, touching too on my parents'
decline. There's also a disclaimer: "the world will not be moved by
words, though poets would have it so"—re Shelley's claim that we
are the "unacknowledged legislators of the world" (See "A Defense

of Poetry," *Percy Bysshe Shelley: Selected Poems and Prose*. Penguin Classics, 2016: 651). I hope, of course, for change toward compassion.

241   **To the edge & back: the gift.** A poem for my former student, poet Melissa Wray, whom I have called a "free verse Sappho." Both she and I "had drunk and seen the spider" (*The Winter's Tale* Arden ed., 2.1.45), and have had to wrestle with similar demons..

242   **New Home.** Jim Cohn notes: his "one bedroom condo on 18th Street between Canyon & Arapaho in central Boulder [was] right along the Farmer's Ditch that peels water from Boulder Creek & delivers it out east to farmers with water rights." The poem moves to the imagination beyond the home's walls to explore the poet's imaginative leaps, his gift to help others, the true meanings of his work while in this home.

243   **Hostas.** Cheated out of his earned retirement funds, a worker is forced to make do with tasks that could never keep up with his bills, his only sanity left remembering fallen comrades.

244   **Abu Ghraib.** A military prison outside Baghdad, where U. S. military personnel routinely tortured Iraqi prisoners, seemingly enjoying their behavior until it was exposed. The Associated Press reported these abuses in 2003, and both CBS *Sixty Minutes* and later the ACLU released filmed portions on the abuse.

245   **After Lope.** Adapted from Lope de Vega's *Rimas Humanos* I, found in *Renaissance and Baroque Poetry of Spain*, ed. Elias Rivers. Charles Scribner's Sons, 1966. Pages 214-215.

246   **Haditha.** Based on news coverage of the Haditha massacre, 19 Nov. 2005.

247   **Desert Serenade.** A tale told to me by a student, who asked me to write a poem commemorating her experience.

248   **Marines with Cobbled Armor.** Based on a live TV report observed on locker room TV after a shower at a local gym.

249   **October Surprise: An Absurd Reverie.** Written per speculation that Republicans would pull an election year stunt just before voting day; sent to Ed Sanders re his request for "October Surprise" poems. Published in his online *Woodstock Journal.*

250   **Rush Hour in the Swamp, Near Hopewell Mounds.** The "Hopewell Mounds" are first people's burial mounds near the Owashtanong (Grand) River, with I-196 freeway on one side and the river and bike trail where I ride on the other. Sacred land near where I live.

251   **May.** Juxtaposition of new graduates reciting a Stevens poem at their commencement and tragedy of a friend killed in motorcycle accident.

252   **Last of My Singing Fathers.** For Carl Rakosi (1903-2004) who insisted that his poems were a kind of realism, that the tag "objectivist" was not sufficient to describe his work, despite his being linked with George Oppen, Charles Reznikoff, Louis Zukofsky, and Lorine Niedecker in that early 1930s poetic movement. The phrase "no poet sitting on his exquisite ass" is from section 3 of "Dream," subtitled "And what were the poets doing then?" (*The Collected Poems of Carl Rakosi.* The National Poetry Foundation/U of Maine, 1986. 299). My poem also recalls "The Old Poet's Tale," written for George Oppen, which Carl read at The Naropa Objectivist Conference.

254   **A Midnight Rose for Michael Pingarron.** An elegy for New Jersey poet Michael Pingarron, with whom I shared a love of Lorca and Neruda. This poem is also a disability poem showing the intense disappointments of a poet teacher denied the right to care for needy students because of prejudice borne of his disability. Pingarron's book, *The Surrealist Explains His Smile: Selected Poems of Michael Pingarron, 1982-2006,* was published posthumously by Dave Roskos's Iniquity Press.

255   Big Sale Shop, Bargains Galore. Antique shop on the road to Frankfort, Mi., near the turnoff for Crystal Lake. Poem notes items being sold—Sue and I pausing before two emblematic prints of Chinese summer mountains.

256   The City in Agony. A summer day in which a murderer ran riot through downtown Grand Rapids, racing the wrong way on US 131, going to home where he held family members hostage, then shot himself, with cops and neighbors, news reporters and those watching it on TV traumatized. See Wikipedia: 2011 Grand Rapids Shootings.

257   Seul Choix Shoreline, Owashtanong Dreams. The only choice for sailors of sinking ships on the south shore of the Upper Peninsula and a declaration invoking the Owashtanong, river passing through my home town.

Frail Dreams 2008

The two suites of this section, "Frail Dreams" for my mother and "Flight to Phoenix" for my father, comprise one of the most sustained poems I have written, following the deaths of my parents, completing paeans and laments for them both. My mother's suite follows her decline and death over a longer period of time, while my father's is a group of poems based on a single visit to see my second mom and to visit his grave. Both sequences include a seminal poem keyed to one's life and place—"A Dream of Jerusalem" for my mom, and "River Rouge" for my dad. Each also has a final poem functioning as a coda, the deaths understood after the passage of time.

Frail Dreams: a suite for my mother (Jean Hamilton Cope, 1923-2008)

261   **As My Mother Lay Waiting.** This poem muses on the perception that we too must eventually go the way that my mother is going, the finality of her passage coming in the not-too-distant future, that we too must eventually go, that my children may be as shaken and struggling with the coming loss, as I was.

262   **Starlight Call.** First clear sign of my mother's decline, syllable jamming employed as a grammar of panic.

263   **Fallen.** Return of her earlier sorrows through her confused behavior.

264   **Death, you come.** A rare use of personification ("Death" as a vivid presence).

266   **Frail Dreams.** Conference with caregivers to plan future steps for her care, given her deteriorating condition.

267   **The black bees.** Outdoor lunch under a pergola, the bees working the flowers on the vines above us. My siblings talk over the lunch, while our mom is oblivious to them, her eyes following the bees intently.

268   **Between Sleep & Wake.** My last birthday with her. I had always made a practice of calling her at 8:35 a.m. on my birthday, the moment I was born. Here, a thanks for giving me birth.

269   **Her New Room.** Her final days, stripped of most of her belongings, more and more "in fitful sleep." A supremely melancholy day, wondering if she'd ever live to appreciate those

belongings we saved for her, or living the illusion that she'd make a new life there, with death so close.

270   **Mais où sont les neiges d'antan?** Some years before, my son Will was given an assignment to interview his grandmother; he proved supremely adept at framing questions for her. She gave him memories that none of us had known before—French lessons with Miss Meloche, or the fact that as a freshman at U of Michigan, she was chosen to speak to a newspaper reporter on what students thought after Pearl Harbor. I found Will's written interview while my mom was dying, and this poem is the result, with the famous refrain in one portion of François Villon's *Le Testament*, rendered in English as "but where are the snows of yesteryear?" Also, "if ya can say it's a bra brecht moonlicht nicht" is from a Scottish song my maternal grandfather used to sing in the mornings or when requested.

271   **Last look.** A simple farewell, sitting with my mother's corpse, kissing her cold forehead and admiring her face one last time.

272   **A Dream of Jerusalem.** Ekphrasis based on Spanish sculptor Jaume Plensa's "Jerusalem," a linear series of gongs with soft hammers nearby, along with encouraging sign to hammer the gongs, on which were engraved quotations from *Song of Songs*. "A Dream of Jerusalem" begins with my own associations with the city through William Blake's prophetic "Jerusalem"—the city itself as metaphor for imaginative redemption—and through childhood reflection on Jerusalem as locus for both spiritual journey and holocaust, the latter including *Lamentations*—the fall of the city, the destruction of the temple, and the Babylonian Captivity—as well as the slaughter of the population and destruction of the second Temple c. 70 CE, as recounted by Josephus in *The Jewish War*.

There were also the countervailing associations: *Song of Songs* is in many ways a woman's book, a book of love and longing, of the spiritual sexuality of love itself, and in thinking about the poem I would write, I recalled the woman's search and the famous refrain in 2:7, 3:5, and 8:4, which I rendered freely as "none may turn to Love until it descends in morning dew and in calling doves." While this line would become the refrain of the poem, I did not initially think of it as such; in the first draft, the line was repeated as the ninth line—it just seemed to fit there—and it came up again as the final line of the poem. Later, I reworked lines in the middle section, largely for condensation of phrasing and specificity of image, and in this process repeated the line as the 21st line, thus framing the poem with two refrains at the beginning (lines 3-4 and 11-12) and two at the end (lines 27-28 and 35-36).

This was immensely satisfying, as I've long been fascinated with the construction of tercet and couplet-based poems—variations on dantescan and ghazal patterns of construction as a kind of weaving. "A Dream of Jerusalem" became a sort of Mexican blanket for me, with the refrains as stripes repeating each other at each end of the blanket. Beyond this pattern, I was fascinated by Plensa's sound hammers and his request that those experiencing the work should take a hammer and hit the gong nearby. More fascinating was the potential for sound and the notion of sound or action moving out in waves which imply changes far beyond the initial action, in Basho's famous "frog kerplunk" poem, for example. I had explored this concept in my 1993 poem "Catching Nothing" (See pages 143-145), which ends with this idea of actions changing the world:

> Even
> our hearts beat like
> hammers now, sending out waves of sound
> over & over—
> the breath
> is a wind that
> stirs up all the world.

When I came to Plensa's notion of the gongs, this binary concept of stillness/action found form in the idea of the shofur untouched and of the "presence that could in a soundless tomb shiver the dark with hammers, sound the call in waves shimmering in all the wheels turning across the universe & make seraphs weep." Silence became the meditative center of the poem, a priori the "unheard music of spheres" that can't be heard in a fallen age.

The last major association was the idea of the woman herself in *Song of Songs*, fairly obviously a young woman in the prime of her youth—yet I also thought of her as the elder she would finally become, of Time itself. I had lost my own mother this year, thus the importance of the child reaching out to touch the mother's cheek, the bone where the mother's vision once stirred, and finally the ashes which "swirl in shining waves, sink into dark murk & are gone"—an image from the final ceremony after my mother's death, wherein my siblings cast my mother's ashes into the river where she raised us. The poem is thus the central poem in the sequence of works exploring my mother's passage from this life and my own self-discovery borne of that passage. In the associations which come from my mother's passing, there is also the image of the "scattered bones chirping in dry day"—that astounding image from the valley of dry bones, wherein the voice asks the prophet whether these bones shall live (*Ezekial* 37:3). The part of my mind that was revolving on the associations with my mother's death picked up on the chirping bones, an image I had previously combined with the notion of Christ as the "word made flesh," turning the phrase in my 1993 poem "For Martin King"—"who sang the flesh made word, that bones may walk." The image returned here as a rebirth, as the city itself has been reborn.

All these associations were activated when I first encountered Plensa's *Jerusalem*. When it came to the composition, the words came quickly. It was as if I already knew them, and of course it had nothing to do with the notion of occasional composition, but rather with *opening oneself* to the associations evoked by the work. The poem fell quite naturally into the pattern of tercets, a format I have been very comfortable with since my extensive interrogation of Dante's *Commedia*. (Note that the poem has since been reformatted and in quatrains, necessitated by the publication format of *The Invisible Keys: New and Selected Poems*). Some minor motifs popped up in the fury of the writing, among these the notion of "blind sight," borne of my years watching Olivier's film of *King Lear*, wherein the mad king sees the world clearly for the first time in his encounter with the blind Gloucester. Other such motifs include the Egyptian notion of the "sun disc's eternal round" and the aforementioned medieval concept of the music of the spheres. The images of the world in crisis, whether brothers crying at the prison door, the women lying in their "last dank beds" or "boys shouldering rifles behind dusty tanks" are generic from the news, yet they're also specific, minute particulars which identify actual events.

274   **Crystal Lake to Beulah.** Northern Michigan lake famed for its clear waters, with the town of Beulah situated at its east end. A morning walk to town, recalling the week before when my siblings and I began an early summer ritual of kayaking to the spot on the Thornapple River where we scattered my mother's ashes, throwing rose petals from my garden on the water. The spot was directly below the great black oak on the moraine above, where my mother used to go and find solace from what her life had become after the divorce from my father. This poem was written a year after her death, and completes the suite for my mother.

Flight to Phoenix: a suite for my father (Robert Edge Cope, 1920-2008.)

The arc of the relationship with my father was very different from the pattern with my mother, and while my reconciliation with my dad was one of the greatest revelations of my life, I was not physically present as he went through his final struggle before death. My mother was across town and it was easier to be present in her final years, while my father had moved with his second wife Betty to Arizona for health reasons. I couldn't afford flights to visit him, and my free time was stretched quite thin with my teaching career, raising my three children, and pursuing my writing career. "River Rouge" is the central poem of this set, forming at once an historical overview of the city of Detroit and my family's, dad's and my place there, with numerous points of memory and departure.

276   **The Swimmer.** My father had been a swimmer for the University of Michigan swim team, and taught me to swim at age 5 in the local YMCA pool, canoed beside me when I did my first half-mile swim on the Thornapple River at age 9. In this poem, he is in a hotel pool, wounded from a hiking fall and quite tentative until he could assume his favorite stroke, elegant and effortless as we all remembered.

277   **Flight to Phoenix.** Dreaming in my seat, recalling how much my face resembled his, how I followed his canoe in my first long swim, as he later followed me up the Bright Angel Trail to the south rim of the Grand Canyon. Second stanza pauses on the suffering we both endured during my estranged youth and middle years; the third measures our passage near Vishnu schist (ancient rock at the canyon's bottom) and at the thousand year old handprint in a Sinagua doorway at the five story Montezuma Castle cliff dwelling.

278   **In My Father's House.** Scenes from my dad's life, including the seven sacred pools of Hana; Longs Peak, Colorado—a dangerous but rewarding climb hazarded by my dad in the 1930s on a trail now closed, and by me in 1990; and Tahquamenon Falls, Paradise, Michigan. Looking out his window, I find myself shaken, realizing he is with me—the experience of memory giving way to a strange visionary moment.

279   The Empty Chair. Visiting my second mom, Betty, after my dad's death. Lunch at Apache Junction burger joint, where we'd gone on an earlier visit when he was with us. There were three of us at a table for four, and the empty chair was somewhat haunting.

280   Tahquamenon. This was my family's first visit to the falls after dad's death, in which I was startled again by his spirit's presence beside me.

281   River Rouge. This poem is in three parts, gradually revealing a much more complex subject than the initial experiment in ekphrasis upon viewing Charles Sheeler's 1932 painting of the mile long Ford factory near Detroit, later the subject of the masterful Detroit Industry Murals by Diego Rivera. In the first part (Faces in Shadow, page 281), I imagined the toxic clouds and their effect on the workers and local folk; I realized that Sheeler had reduced the plant to its outlines, so I brought the thousands of workers' "out of the shadow" and showed them on the job—their initial morning chatter quickly subsumed in the roar of the machines, forcing them into robotic movements in the assembly lines, the bosses measuring their performances. As a one-time factory worker, I knew this pattern intimately, and of course Rivera's murals show clearly what Sheeler had ignored.

The second part (Beyond the Shadow, page 282) brings my family into the light: my father growing up in Detroit, while my grandfather worked at Con Ed, their world divisible by day (kids jumping off roofs) and by night (the Purple Gang shooting it out with the FBI), my dad swinging to the sounds of Duke Ellington and Benny Goodman. Their world was punctuated by the Battle of the Overpass, where Ford's goons beat Walter Reuther until his skull bled. There were also the race rebellions of 1943, where my newly married dad had to lock my mom into their apartment, passing machine gun emplacements at major intersections on his way to work as a metallurgical engineer designing parts for the weapons allied troops would need to win World War II.

The third part (The Scythe, page 283) expands the frame of reference to the city itself and its people, caught in the Scythe of Time. Finally, the poem is a tale of Time and the folk who inhabit the dreams in a city, with my grandfather, my dad and I exemplars of lives passed and passing. It serves as an overview of my dad's whole life, from childhood to his passing. In this suite of poems; it functions in a way similar to the way "A Dream of Jerusalem does in the suite of elegies for my mother.

285   **Happy birthday: you'd be 99.** As with "Crystal Lake to Beulah" in the sequence of elegies for my mother, this poem was written some years after the initial group for my father, imparting some perspective to the processes of grief.

September Moon 2009-2013

September Moon covers my final years as a professor at Grand Rapids Community College, my years also as Grand Rapids Poet Laureate. This section discloses my fascination with life changes; these are also the first mature poems of my career. There are elegies for friends–notably guitarist composer Frank Salamone, a college friend and gifted musician, and a gesture of remembrance for my mother, scattering roses from my garden on the spot where my family cast her ashes in the Thornapple River. Also, Meijer Gardens and Sculpture Park engaged six local poets to create poetry based on the works of sculptor Jaume Plensa, resulting in ekphrasis poems; their little anthology of our work was published for an audience of local literati and members of the Gardens. I had long been fascinated with ekphrasis as an approach to poetry, and thought to engage my creative writing students in a writing exercise based on paintings by Modigliani and Picasso (see "Emile at the Crossroads, page 290 and the notes on that poem) and wrote my own poem with them. Later, I was engaged by the Grand Rapids Art Museum to select one of their featured artworks, write about it, and sit nearby with copies of the poem I produced, reading it aloud to all who wanted to hear it. I thus wrote about "American Pewter with Burroughs II" a Robert Rauschenberg masterpiece and for me, another ekphrasis poem.

289   **Andrei Voznesensky.** An elegy for the poet (1933-2010). "I am Goya" and "Darkmotherscream," are from translations which appeared in *20th Century Russian Poetry: Silver and Steel*, ed. Yevgeny Yevtushenko.

290   **Emile at the Crossroads.** This was the ekphrastic writing exercise I engaged in with my creative writing students, involving placing a young red-haired girl in a Modigliani painting side by side with a haunted old man painted by Picasso on the chalk tray at the front of the room. Students could write on one of these two or on both, and I wrote my own poem. After 15 minutes or so, I asked them if they'd like to recite their poems, and at the end of their works, I recited this, my poem. They were curious about the subject, so I shared my long studies of the second world war, with the haunting images of mass murders perpetrated by the Nazis in eastern Europe before they hit on the idea of setting up gas chambers to kill on a more industrial scale.

291   **March.** Free form ghazal, this poem initially details the effects of recession—foreclosures, job loss, "fat cats disappearing after shanking the economy." The poem turns to the many deaths I'd struggled with in recent years, a need for tenderness after "so much death & sorrow." Kayaking across the river to scatter rose petals on the spot where we placed my mother's ashes the year before was such a moment, in spite of the "procession of the dead. . . their fragile memory all that remains."

292   **She.** A confession and paean to my beloved, Suzanne. "unicorn and millefleurs": her needlepoint based on the Unicorn Tapestries in the Cloisters (NYC), still gracing the central spot in our living

room after 54 years. "given language to those with none": her enormous skill in tutoring children in need. 'little flower": St. Therese of Lisieux. "rosa mundi": rose of the world. "neither little flower nor rosa mundi": avoiding categories, simply seeing the need for healing in others and helping them find their way.

294   **April.** Moraine: cliffs plowed up on the sides of riverbeds by retreating glaciers during the last ice age.

295   **The Crippled Doe.** Kayaking apart from my companions on Big Manistee River, a gesture with a wounded deer.

296   **Two for Creeley.** Elegy for Robert Creeley (1926-2005) written as homage in his style of verse. Two sections: one based on a memory of lending my copy of *For Love* to a friend, ending with a Creeleyesque line, and the other subtitled with his book that influenced me most, *words*, and my memory of postcards he'd sent me with brief congratulations and his signature salute, "Onward," the poem concluding with a turn to images of regenerative spring.

298   **Blues for Frank.** Blues elegy for my friend Frank Salamone, a locally famous blues guitarist and composer. The poem is loaded with blues and folk-rock titles and musicians, as well as references to Frank's disease. Frank and I first met when we were co-editors of Grand Rapids Junior College's writing and arts magazine, *Display*. We became notorious for Frank's use of the word "fuck" in his story, while I employed "Goddamn" in my poem; we were censured by the Faculty Senate via two professors who were religious cranks and wanted us and our faculty advisor, Walter Lockwood, taken to task. We were defended on the grounds of freedom of expression by our department chair, Marinus Swets, and allowed to remain in school. Later, I married and Frank had been married, then divorced, and lived down the street from us. I had become enamored of the Rolling Stones' interpretations of songs by Howlin' Wolf, Muddy Waters, Robert Johnson, and Slim

Harpo, among others, and Frank began sharing his enormous musical knowledge borne of the Delta Blues and folk music with me. In short, he educated me in these key American musical forms; eventually, I expanded my loves to other black music traditions, notably jazz and Motown. We appeared in each other's lives off and on to the time of his passing, and this elegy was my contribution to his rosary service and a concert on his behalf by other blues guitarists who deeply valued his work.

References in this poem: "a pigfoot and a bottle of beer"—one of Bessie Smith's iconic songs. "money maker"—from "Shake Your Money Maker" by Elmore James. M.S.—multiple sclerosis, the debilitating disease that took Frank's gift from him. "skeletones"—a local blues group. Doehler-Jarvis—a factory where the men of Frank's family worked. Woody Guthrie through John Renbourn—great songwriters and guitarists in the blues and folk traditions. "rent party rag"—rent parties raised funds so that the apartment dweller could pay the rent when he/she couldn't afford it; Spider John Koerner's version of the song was the one we knew. "wang dang doodle"—song about a wild party made famous by Howlin' Wolf. "careless love"—"O love, O love, O careless love," a blues performed by many musicians over the years. "police dog blues"—a song by Blind Blake. "hellhounds"—the great Robert Johnson's most famous song, "Hellhound on My Trail." "midnight special—Leadbelly's "Let the Midnight Special shine its everlovin' light on Me"; The Midnight Special was a train that passed the prison where Leadbelly was incarcerated every night about midnight, a sign of his freedom-to-come. "We shall not be moved"—the famous gospel and civil rights song. "hang it on the wall"—song by the legendary bluesman, Charley Patton.

300   **American Pewter with Burroughs II.** Ekphrasis based on images selected from Robert Rauschenberg's work of the same name. References: "green man leafy head"—character in the tradition of medieval vegetation deities who must die so that he may be reborn

the following year. Examples range from the poem "Sir Gawain and the Green Knight" to the sculpture of the green man in the cathedral of Bamberg, Germany. Quotes in Stanza 1 are from William S. Burroughs' son Billy, in "Fury is a Sign of Life," published in *New Blood*. Ed. Tom Swartz and Michael Wojczuk. Artz Press, 1980. Sappho: reference is to the poem translated by Mary Barnard as "To an Army Life in Sardis," and as #16, following the Greek more precisely in Diane Rayor's translation. Iron worker in the Rauschenberg collage is here transformed as a green man. The iron worker and the Greek warriors are present in the artist's book, *Rauschenberg at Gemini*. Armory Center for the Arts, 2010. 30-31.

301   **For Antler, after the storm.** For my dear friend, author of the epic environmental poem *Factory* and of *Last Words*. Madeleine Island is in Lake Superior, sacred island in Anishinaabe mythos. El Capitan is the famed Peak in Yosemite National Park. Audubon is a 13,200 ft. mountain in Colorado. I have climbed this mountain twice, once with Antler who stripped naked and bowed to the sun atop the summit. Jeff is Jeff Poniewaz, poet, environmental activist, and classical music critic, Antler's life companion.

302   **Thornapple.** Commitment of my mother's ashes in the waters of the Thornapple River below her former bedroom window, a rite that led to my brother and me kayaking to that spot every June for years, that we might cast rose petals from my garden on the waters as a form of remembrance.

303   **So the day begins.** From lapping waves to laughter of friends– finale of this section.

The Gateless Gate 2014-2016

This section is transitional from my labors as a professor to the realignment of my priorities, this book among them. It opens with two ekphrasis poems, but features my sailing to Milwaukee to read at Woodland Pattern Books and to spend time with Antler and Jeff Poniewaz, two poets whom I published in *Big Scream* for years. Jeff was in his final days, yet found time to ask the owner of Woodland Pattern to bring me there. The two Milwaukee poems involve discussions with Jeff on Milwaukee and those who've visited or written about it, all this while Antler played piano to entertain us at their apartment. The second poem is my elegy for Jeff after he passed. There are 6 elegies in this book, the presence of death as a recurring reminder as one ages. The section ends with a trip to Chicago to teach my non-binary adult child Alex's class how to read Allen Ginsberg's *Howl*, the first of my major poems in my life as an elder.

307   **I, You, She or He.** Ekphrasis based on Jaume Plensa's sculptural installation at Frederik Meijer Gardens and Sculpture Park experience shared with poet Linda Nemec Foster and Meijer representative Heidi Holst.

308   **A Language of Our Time.** Ekphrasis based on six pieces by Hanneke Beaumont at Frederik Meijer Sculpture Gardens and Sculpture Park. Three of these moved me, inspiring this poem.

311   **Wyrd Song.** "Wyrd"—Old English, from "Eard-Stapa" (The Wanderer): Wyrd bith ful anraed (Fate be fully resolute). A poem of crossing Lake Michigan in fog, early spring, with ruminations drawn from Denise Levertov's great pro-peace poem, "Staying Alive," "wondering how we all survived the *sturm-und-drang* of those years," dreaming of the obscured shore ahead.

312   **Early Spring Morn Milwaukee** "Diotima" is a woman philosopher in Plato's *Symposium* who recommended that in post-

child raising age, men should cultivarte relationships with younger men. "Maurice" is the hero of E. M. Forster's novel of the same name. "Margaret Fuller" is a transcendentalist and early American feminist, who visited Milwaukee and other points on the Great Lakes, exploring the conditions women lived with in her 1843 prose work, *Summer on the Lakes*, a classic text of early American feminism.

314   **Adieu à Jeff Because.** "Because": Jeff's surname "Poniewaz" translates to "Because" in English. "ecopoetics raindance rendezvous": the summer 1990 Ecopoetics Conference at Naropa Institute, Boulder, Co. The phrase plays on two other events: a Native American raindance, a ceremony intended to bring rain to a parched region, and the "rendezvous," an annual gathering of mountain men in the 19th century, which occasioned wild celebrations after hard winters—the poets here as modern mountain men and women with friends they'd not seen for some time. "Gaia" is the living spirit of the earth itself, per the Gaia hypothesis. "Muir & Leopold": John Muir and Aldo Leopold are two pillars of environmental awareness, both originally from Wisconsin. Jeff was a leader in the fight to save the Milwaukee riverfront from commercial developers.

315   **Dawn Kayaking the Owashtanong.** A healing poem for Curt Jordan, who had returned to Grandville from Seattle for his grandfather's funeral.

318   **Rix is Gone.** Gifted New Jersey poet Bob Rixon, friend and dialogue partner since the early 1980s, his work never properly collected in a volume despite his gift. This elegy mourns his passing.

319   **End at the Beginning.** Elegy for my oldest friend, John Breidenfield, elder brother to Billy, whose struggles with ALS are found earlier in these poems. John succumbed to the disease as

well; I knew him and loved him from the second grade onward. "Voyageurs" were 17th century explorers and missionaries who came up the St. Lawrence River to explore the Great Lakes and points beyond, doing business and attempting to convert Native nations to their religion.

320   **The Gateless Gate.** Title: see this book of koans used as spiritual practice for zen students. *Two Zen Classics: Mumonkan and Hekiganroku.* Trans. with commentaries by Katsuki Sekida. Weatherhill, 1977. Pages 25-27. Final service for Suzanne's mother, said at the grave by son, Msgr. Ernest Schneider, my brother-in-law, Suzanne, her sister Cathy, and me.

321   **May Song.** On the trails and at home, before campfires breathing in the Spring.

322   **The Work.** Coming home from trail ride to planting in garden.

323   **"the weight of the world is love."** This title is the two opening lines of Allen Ginsberg's early poem "Song." Charleston 9 were African American worshippers murdered at prayer meeting by a racist, 17 June 2015. "care came for the poor"—funding for Planned Parenthood clinics that serve poor women. "marital bliss . . . denied, the doors opened"—LGBTQ+ marriages made legal.

324   **Leaves in Fall.** Stop-the-world silent meditation.

325   **long thin clouds.** Flight to Minneapolis/St. Paul where I celebrated Chinese New Year with poet Wang Ping, meeting and reading with two of her classes at Macalester College.

326   **For Anne at 70.** Paean to Anne Waldman on her birthday. "TAs" are teaching assistants. Friends and students: Jim Cohn, Chris Ide, Morgan Jarema. Kali Yuga is the dark age we are now entering.

328   **Minneapolis Airport Delay.** Delay in July 6 flight to Phoenix, where I would meet my sister Laurie, visit my dad's grave and spend time with my second mom. Aleppo is a city gutted in the Syrian civil war. Also, numerous cases of black men murdered by police make a pattern far too familiar to Americans. "nightly news replays" are horrific news stories from the 1960s. "Castile family": family of Philando Castile, a black man shot to death by policeman in Falcon Heights, MN, suburb of St. Paul not far from the airport.

329   **The Train: *Howl* in Chicago.** Seven movements:

329   *Prologue.* Quotation by Allen Ginsberg is from a 1978 interview by James Mackenzie in *First Thought: Conversations with Allen Ginsberg.* Ed. Michael Schumacher. U of Minnesota, 2017. Alex, my non-binary adult child, was teaching an afternoon AP high school class in Chicago and asked me to join the class for a discussion of *Howl.* Traveling on the train, my mind filled with memories of Allen's significance as a poet and cultural figure, also wondering whether the students would have the wherewithal to grasp the particulars of the poem, or if they'd see what it can do for those with curious minds.

330   *Kalamazoo thru the farmlands.* Prague, "open consciousness," *First Thought*, 14-17.

331   *Michigan City to Calumet, on to Gary.* "branches broken off as in Dante's Hell" refers to *Inferno* XIII: 31-45, where the spirit is Pier della Vigna. "Allen joked he'd be in a cottage 20 years after *Howl*": Kostelanetz, in *First Thought*, 22. "Blake singing on his death-bed" is from Chesterton, G. K. *William Blake.* Reprint ed. Create-Space Independent Publishing Platform, 2013. 69-70. Bobby Rixon: reference is to his poems in *Nada Poems.* Ed. David Cope. Nada, 1988. 88-91. Also, "Mimosa." *The Strand.* Chapbook. Nada, 1983. "Fern Hill." is Dylan Thomas's famed syllabic poem of youth, "as I was young and easy in the mercy of his means, Time held me green and dying, though I sang in my chains like the sea." *The Poems of Dylan Thomas.* New Directions, 1971. 195-96.

332   ***Union Station: waiting out the time.*** Three hour wait after arrival in Chicago, then taxi ride to Alex's school. This section of the poem makes a change in style to brief vignettes, observations of others in the great room at the station.

333   ***A Howling Time.*** Meeting Alex's class, recognizing they needed historical examples to grasp Allen's lines. Grant Park police riots: Chicago 1968 Democratic National Convention. Chris Clay: place keywords Chris E. Clay when prompted at the online Wall of Faces Vietnam War. Bill Shields— Vietnam veteran poet, whose work explored both his experiences in war and his intense struggles with PTSD. His chapbook is *NAM*. Long Beach: P.O. Press, n.d. My Bosnian student: in lieu of the required research paper, she wrote a personal essay on the horrors she experienced in their war, submitted it for the college's literary magazine, where she won recognition for her effort. Also, particulars of current life in US contribute to this need for a howling time.

334   ***The Dream.*** Style shift, continuation of motif of personae by which humans find their way through the various ages in life.

335   ***Monroe to Canal on Foot.*** "red line"is a train to downtown Chicago. Get off at Monroe and hike across downtown to Canal, thence to Union Station. The river itself/Marquette/Kaskaskians/ Ludington: Sawyers, June. "Pere Marquette Makes a Chicago 'First.'" *The Chicago Tribune.* 2 April 1989. *Howl on trial*—collection of documents clarifying the famed *Howl* obscenity trial, ed. Bill Morgan. *First Thought*—volume of Allen Ginsberg interviews, ed. Michael Schumacher. "City of Big Shoulders"—from Carl Sandberg's 1914 poem, "Chicago."

These are the poems of my elder years, notably featuring my trip to China as the only American poet among international poets invited to the Suining International Poetry Week, a life-changing event that gave me some sense of my entire career. This new awareness inspired my publication of *A Bridge Across the Pacific: Leaves for Chen Zi'ang, Guan Yin, and Du Fu* (Chicago: Jabber, 2019). This travelogue to China included daily entries, poems written during the visit, photos from Suining and elsewhere, meditations based on my experiences there, and an extensive annotated list of sources I consulted for the trip. The following year, I published *The Invisible Keys: New and Selected Poems.* (Madison, Wi.: Ghost Pony, 2019). This led to readings at Nassau Community College in Garden City, N.Y., to the East Setauket Community House, a visit the Walt Whitman birthplace, and later on to visit old friend James Ruggia, who had organized a reading for Jim Cohn and me, with numerous east coast friends taking their places as readers as well. Among these were Eliot Katz and Andy Clausen, both recovering from difficult medical conditions. All of us were reunited from our years at Naropa and Brooklyn and our shared love of Allen Ginsberg, who had arranged readings and introduced us to each other in years past. Finally, I published *The Correspondence of David Cope & Allen Ginsberg 1976-1996* (Freeport, N.Y.: Giant Steps, 2021.) The shadow of American politics, the concern with aging and its effects, the war in Ukraine, and the loss of friends also contributed to this set.

339   **Kali Yuga Super Blue Blood Moon.** Kali Yuga—the dark age we now inhabit, a time of violence and cruelty, in which poets should keep their lights burning in the Moisopholon Domos (Translation from Greek: house of the muses), awaiting a better time. Super Blue Blood Moon: 31 January 2018.

340   **The Mountain: Inauguration 2017.** Allen Ginsberg's dedication is from "Song." Standing Rock is a Sioux reservation, site of protest to stop Dakota Access oil pipeline from crossing their lands, to protect waterways and lands from oil invasion and

pollution. "women warriors": the Women's March on Washington on 21 January 2017, to protest anti-feminist and anti-woman stance taken by Trump. The Washington march involved over 470,000 people, and other protests in the USA that day attracted between 3.2-5.2 million others; there were 673 marches worldwide. "lamp by the golden door" is from "The Colossus," poem on the Statue of Liberty, the last five lines of which read:

> Give me your tired, your poor,
> Your huddled masses yearning to breathe free,
> The wretched refuse of your teeming shore.
> Send these, the tempest-tost to me,
> I lift my lamp beside the golden door!

341   **Fragile Moves.** A poem for a close friend trapped in grief and regret, rousing me to send her healing thoughts, even as I was reminded of my own regrets and faults, realizing we both needed to seek calm waters and shores.

342   **Flight to Paumanok: A Still Station.** Trip to Paumanok (Long Island) to visit my friend Carmen Bugan and her family, to read and lecture at Nassau Community College in Garden City and at the East Setauket Community House, later to visit the Walt Whitman birthplace.

343   **Manhattan from Jersey City.** Reunion with old friends who I met too seldom since our meetings in the 1980s and 1990s, including my best friends Jim Cohn and James Ruggia, Eliot Katz and Danny Shot. I also met younger poets in the coffee shop near the park and the view of Manhattan. Quote from Allen Ginsberg ("Man City, my city") is from "Bayonne Entering NYC" (page 37 in City Lights Paperback, in *Collected Poems 1947-1997*, page 428).

344   **After the Polar Vortex.** Polar vortex is a great swath of frigid air that, if unbalanced from its usual circular pattern around the pole,

dips south and wreaks havoc with temperate zone weather. We had such a vortex in January 2019 before I had to take the train to the Chinese Embassy in Chicago to apply for a passport for the Suining International Poetry Week in Sichuan. This poem is a narrative of that journey in the frozen darkness, dreaming of the many folk and animals watching us pass, as well as musing on the spirits of that convention of poets: Du Fu, China's greatest poet (712-770 CE), who took refuge in a thatched hut in Chengdu, fleeing the constant warfare that marked his life and finding solace there for a few years before having to flee again, victim of more organized violence. Also, Guan Yin, Buddhist goddess of mercy, and Chen Zi'ang (658-701 CE), born in She-hong but claimed by Suining, the forerunner of T'ang poetry who spoke truth to power when he couldn't disentangle himself from court politics. The poem turns at this point to making a vow to honor my hosts and my own nation, to keep a compassionate and kind heart. The final movement returns to the dream as the train moves onward, bringing me to the destination that would make my journey to China possible as the only American poet in the group of international poets invited to the conference. See *A Bridge Across the Pacific: Leaves for Chen Zi'ang, Guan Yin, and Du Fu.* (Jabber, 2019). For further documentation, see Bill Porter/Red Pine. *Finding Them Gone: Visiting China's Poets of the Past.* Port Townsend, Washington: Copper Canyon, 2016. Also, David Young. *Du Fu: A Life in Poetry.* New York: Knopf, 2019.

347 **The Moon.** This poem begins with the full moon lighting the forest, followed by what I knew of the journeys and lives of Chen Zi'ang and Du Fu, each of them leaving home and comfort for the journey beyond.

348 **Waiting for dawn in a Beijing hotel room.** Late at night in my room after a 13 hour flight from Chicago, recalling that part of the journey—my first poem in China. I followed my thoughts, with two stanzas musing on what I knew in March 2019 of Du Fu and

Chen Zi'ang, thence to age and regret, the quiet dance one performs as one approaches death. This ends with remembrance of a young Chinese mother who was traveling with her baby, pleased to talk with me as we awaited our flight.

349 **From the top step of Guangde Temple.** A poem written at 4 a.m. on my first night in Sichuan, musing on the events of my first day in Suining. The poem went through several revisions before breakfast at 6 a.m. It was revised again in 2021 when my translator Zhang Ziqing suggested that the second word in the final line ("gong") should be revised with the actual instrument used to call the people to worship. After several exchanges, we both agreed that it would be OK to translate the word as "dharma fish," a wooden fish actually used by the monks as a call to service.

350 **A Song for Our Lady.** A poem on the burning of the Cathedral of Notre Dame de Paris, 15 April 2019. My sources include The PBS documentary *Saving Notre Dame* and conversations I had with Professor Jacqueline Jung, Yale art historian renowned for her knowledge of cathedrals and their statuary. I wrote this, too, for the many generations of common people who found a home full of sustenance and spirituality in this great ship of the spirit.

351 **Memory's Balm.** The Thornapple, river of my childhood, in flood: I crossed to the island and cabin home of Tom Clay with friends not seen in decades, knowing that this night would be a night for memory, a night of collective healing. Tom, Celia, and John Clay, Craig MacIntyre and Tom's daughter Amy all shared their home and a fabulous grilled salmon dinner, welcoming me as an honored guest. After dinner, we sat around the fireplace, and at their request I read my elegies for their brothers, my best friends in our teen years: Chris Clay, who was killed in Vietnam, and Craig's brothers, Todd and Scott. As a poet, this was a night and recitation unlike any other I have experienced.

352   **Beyond the dream, the open door.** An elegy for Sue's uncle Pete, wounded in the European theatre of World War II, as was her dad (see "Antietam," page 59). Like many other veteran survivors of that war, he never talked about his experiences until his final years, when he must have needed to unburden himself of haunting memories. This is my paean for him, and for those other veterans from that war whom I knew via their visits to Lincoln pool when I was pool attendant: quiet, gallant men enjoying their time together.

353   **Among the best minds of his generation.** My student Lisa McAllister named her son after Allen Ginsberg, and this poem follows my experience of this precocious child's friends and relatives' sorrows at his memorial service. The youths' agonies awakened my empathy for this generation's confusion at this new sense of loss, via my own experiences with my friends' early deaths.

354   **A Desperate Mother.** Empty shelves and coolers, crippled supply chain one of the effects of covid, and here a mother who'd been unable to find milk for her child in the grocery store.

355   **Unbidden Dream: a melancholy evening, calm & free.** Meditation on the regrets, illusions, memory loss, illuminations, appearing when least expected, surrounded too by spirits, the melancholy of aging, with blessings of kousa flowers: The title is both a serious moment in my life and a lightly satiric comment on Wordsworth's poem "It is a Beauteous Evening, calm and free."

357   **Alvin Ailey's Ode.** The famed Alvin Ailey dance troupe played the legendary Auditorium Theatre in Chicago just as the covid pandemic began its first surge in the Midwest. We attended a spirited performance of my favorite dance troupe with my sister Laurie, her husband Mark, their daughter and ours. Ailey's "Ode" was the second piece by resident choreographer Jamar Roberts—his paean and lament for the victims of gun violence. Filmed versions of the dance place a male dancer in the role of hero and victim, yet our show presented a gifted woman in the role, the dance leading from death and lament to awakening and resurrection.

358 **Chicago Springtime.** Companion poem to "Alvin Ailey's Ode." I wrote this in the common room of the B & B where we were staying, turning to a photo of Picasso and other writers and artists celebrating the liberation of Paris from the Nazi scourge.

359 **Silent March Candlelight Vigil for George Floyd.** Floyd was murdered by police on 25 May 2020. On 30 May 2020, this march in Grand Rapids, Mi. was one of many marches on or around this date and afterwards. All locations in the poem are in this downtown where it became anything but silent. References: "boogaloo bois": far right extremist group(s) involved in violent anti-government riots in US during this period; see the Southern Poverty Law Center's year-by-year charts detailing known hate groups. "Agents provocateurs": in the late 60s, government agents dressed as hippies, who incited violence before news cameras to convince TV audiences that the protestors were doing it. Allen Ginsberg obtained Freedom of Information papers and sat with me after his reading in Baltimore, going over redacted communiques written by these agents to their superiors, in this case the sections covering Detroit and Ann Arbor. Last six lines, an extended turn with a prayer to dead George Floyd: "peaceful spirit, be with us now."

360 **Love in the Corona.** The opening statement and question set the theme—"Turn off the news . . . where does one find love in this sunrise with its promise?" Despite my garden's beauty, the memory of friends' deaths, my translator Zhang Ziqing's prescient warning speaks of pandemic horror in China, yet there's a turn to adjustment (Italians singing on balconies, Scandinavian knitters blogging their show). Turn to modernists demanding contact—as in *Contact*—a modernist magazine founded by William Carlos

Williams and Robert McAlmon, providing contact via publication for Pound, Stein, WCW, Hemingway, etc.—perhaps a model of what was lost in the pandemic, the necessary item to rebuild a fractured community. After *Contact*, "the sullen art," in Dylan Thomas's poem "In My Craft or Sullen Art": sullen is understood as solitary. All these references function in a different way in the pandemic—the poem turns at last to my casual proposal to Suzanne, 50 years before, on the Ides of March, 1970.

361   **January 6 Suite.** Five movements:

361   ***Out of the Shadow.*** A poem in tercets, listing the apocalyptic horrors of the year, all the incitements to rage, and my confession of failure to practice ahimsa, finding one's way to the light of compassion and kindness.

362   ***Day of Liberation.*** Poem begins with a line from Martha and the Vandellas' "Dancing in the Street," as the votes in Philadelphia put Biden over the top in the presidential election, with rising hopes for all those oppressed by the previous administration. Action for Childhood Arrivals: US policy of giving undocumented children the right to remain in the nation and petition for citizenship: a policy stopped during the Trump administration, to be given new life by Joe Biden's presidency.

363   ***Let All Storms Bring Healing Rain.*** Attempts to overturn the legitimate election results, Rudy Giuliani taking the role of Sejanus to Trump's Tiberius (see Suetonius, the chapter on Tiberius in *The Twelve Caesars* for the tale of the obsequious but utterly self-interested and ruthless second-in-command to the cruel emperor, or Ben Jonson's tragedy, *Sejanus*, as well as the PBS series, *I, Claudius*, for the episodes dealing with Tiberius and Sejanus.) "Whitmer, Benson and Nessel": governor, secretary of state, and attorney general of Michigan were all threatened by right-wing thugs, but stood their ground and responded with grace.

364   *A Day.* Title and first line: President Roosevelt's famed response to the attack on Pearl Harbor; the events of January 6, 2021 are in many ways comparable to those of December 7, 1941—perfidy, betrayal, cruelty on full display in the invasion of the capitol and this attempt to overthrow democracy. Invocation of the "better angels" of our nature is from Abraham Lincoln's first inaugural address, wherein he called on the "mystic chords of memory" to bring the nation together out of chaos via our better angels.

365   *Stillness, Silence.* The ordinary beauty of the garden after snowstorm signals the return of everyday loveliness, necessary after the *Sturm und drang* of the greater world and the US election.

366   **Onward, as Creeley Used to Sign.** Robert Creeley occasionally corresponded with me via postcard; he usually completed his message by signing "onward." "Kali Yuga": See: "in Hinduism, . . . the fourth and worst of the four yugas (epochs or ages extending 4.1 to 8.2 billion years in a Yuga Cycle).The Kali Yuga may be the present age, which is full of conflict; "Kali" means 'strife,' 'discord,' 'quarrel,' or 'contention'; Kali Yuga is associated with the demon Kali."

367   **Until Love Is Equal.** A poem written for LGBT+ folk to honor their loves, recited on a local community TV station.

368   **Passing Phantoms.** References: Mission to Mars approaching landing: January 2022. Lines 2-9: sunset fantasy, those who've died (gone west) to be among the music of the spheres—a conflation of my own favorite campfire memories, First Peoples' dreams of meeting their elders after death, and the Pythagorean notion of the music of the spheres generated by the movement of the celestial bodies, inaudible in a fallen age. Lines 10-19: youthful pleasures shoveling snow on 600 ft. driveway through the forest, returning to the dream journey.

369   **Hour of the Ghost Dance.** List as mantra of species believed extinct, followed by climate change, fires and storms, with turn at the end. "Crown of Creation": religious presumption that the world is ours to do with as we please—this attitude a major cause of irresponsible behaviors leading to environmental pollution, destructive actions, etc. "Hetch-Hetchy presumptions": the drowning of the Hetch-Hetchy valley to create a reservoir for San Francisco, contributing to draining of rivers and climate change. Opposed by John Muir in his later years (1907-1913), this first public US environmental controversy destroyed the valley, drove off Native American populations, and serves as a major example of the "crown of creation" mentality.

370   **Ukraine.** A response to the Russian invasion of Ukraine: Whitmanic long-lined litany of horrific battles and written works glorifying the horrors of battle, turning to the perpetrators of wars with the questions asking what drives leaders like these to such cruelties they display. The poem then assumes a first-person meditation on the moon, "wondering at such tranquility tossed for nightmares." The final lines move to a third person narrator, the "I" transformed to "the old man" lost without his futile hope of peace. After this litany of horrors, the Coda to the poem lays blessings on the many folk of Ukraine, the memory of such great Ukrainian poets as Anna Akhmatova and Vasyl Stus, with the hope that the nation might transcend the violent present for a hopeful future. See my essay, "War and Violence, Poetry and Unacknowledged Legislators," in *A Bridge Across the Pacific: Leaves For Chen Zi'ang, Guan Yin, and Du Fu*, and Simone Weil's important treatise, *The Iliad, or the Poem of Force*.

372   **Sanctuary.** A poem retreating to my microworld, caring for three tiny chrysanthemums, that they might live through the cold winter in the unheated greenhouse, to live fully in the coming spring.

373 **Birthday Dreams for Andy.** A paean and birthday wish to poet Andy Clausen on his 80th birthday. Having lost the love of his life, Pamela Twining, then suffering the loss of his leg at the knee, I sent what hopes I could for him, the greatest poet of my generation and a man whose inner strength has given him the will to transcend the suffering for the spirit that animated his consciousness.

374 **Spirit Walk Sunset.** Companion poem to "Passing Phantoms." Poem begins at sunset borne of western wildfires' environmental degradation, funerals via covid, and on the ride home, ending with the question of tomorrows.

377 **Notes**

437 **Acknowledgements**

441 **Index of Titles**

453 **About David Cope**

Acknowledgements

Thanks to the following publishers of my poems over the course of my career and to their editors for supporting my work.

Books

Quiet Lives. Foreword by Allen Ginsberg. Clifton, New Jersey: Humana, 1983.
On the Bridge. Clifton, New Jersey: Humana, 1986
Fragments from the Stars. Clifton, New Jersey: Humana, 1990.
Coming Home. Totowa, New Jersey: Humana, 1993.
Silences f-or Love. Totowa, New Jersey: Humana, 1998.
Turn the Wheel. Totowa, New Jersey: Humana, 2003.
The Invisible Keys: New and Selected Poems. Madison, Wi.: Ghost Pony, 2018.
A Bridge Across the Pacific: Leaves for Chen Zi'ang, Guan Yin, and Du Fu. Chicago: Jabber, 2019.
The Correspondence of David Cope & Allen Ginsberg 1976-1996. Freeport, N.Y. : Giant Steps, 2021.

Chapbooks

Poems from *Moonlight Rose in Blue. David Cope at the Scarab/Detroit.* Grandville, Mi.: Nada, 2009.
Masks of Six Decades: poems 2003-2010. Grandville, Mi.: Nada, 2010.
The Train: Howl *in Chicago.* Ed. George Drury. Chicago: Multifarious Press, 2017.

Anthologies

"Crash." *The Pushcart Prize II: Best of the Small Presses.* Ed. Bill Henderson. Avon, 1978.
Two Poems and Fragments, Ginsberg's choice. *New Directions Anthology #37.* Ed. J. Laughlin, with Peter Glassgold and Frederick R. Martin. New Directions, 1978.

Five Poems. *City Lights Journal #4*. Selection by Allen Ginsberg. Ed. Mendes
    Monsanto. San Francisco: City Lights, 1978.

"Modern Art" and "Party Talk." *Friction 5/6: Obscure Genius Issue*. Ed. Allen
    Ginsberg and Randy Roark. Laocoon, 1984.

"Sirens & Flashing Lights Stop." *Poems for the Nation*. Ed. Allen Ginsberg,
    Andy Clausen, Eliot Katz. New York: Seven Stories, 2000.

Three poems. *Hazmat Review: The Beat Issue*. Ed. Norm Davis. Rochester,
    N. Y.: Clevis Hook, 2000.

"Labor Day." *Visiting Walt: Poems Inspired by the Life and Work of Walt
    Whitman*. Ed. Sheila Coghill and Thom Tammaro. Iowa City: Iowa
    UP, 2003.

"Crash." *Poems to Live By in Troubling Times* Ed. Joan Murray. Boston:
    Beacon, 2006.

"The Rhododendron." *The Grand Rapids Press."* Section J: Your Life. Sunday,
    April 6, 2009. Page 2.

15 poems. *Sins and Felonies*. Ed. G. F. Korreck. Grand Rapids: Barbaric
    Yawp,, 2007.

"A Dream of Jerusalem." *Poetry & Sculpture: Poetry based on the works of
    sculptor Jaume Plensa*. Grand Rapids: Frederik Meijer Gardens, 2008.

Selection of poems. *Fresh Grass*. Ed. Roseanne Ritzema. Rockford: Presa,
    2009.,

9 poems. *Song of the Owashtanong: Grand Rapids Poetry in the 21st Century*. Ed.
    David Cope. Roseville: Ridgeway, 2013.

"the dharma at last." *Poetry in Michigan/Michigan in Poetry*. Ed. William Olsen
    and Jack Ridl. Kalamazoo: New Issues, 2013.

"River Rouge." *Long Poem Masterpieces of the Postbeats*. Ed. Jim Cohn.
    Napalm Health Spa, 2013. Online.

"The Return." *Great Falls/Passaic River Anthology*. Ed. Maria Mazziotti Gillan.
    Paterson: PCCC, 2014.

"For Anne at 70." *Napalm Health Spa Special Edition 2015: Anne Waldman /
    Keeping the World Safe for Poetry*. Ed. Jim Cohn and Eleni Sikileanos.
    Napalm Health Spa, 2015. Online.

Essay on Postbeat Poets and my work "What Thou Lovest Well." By Zhang
    Ziqing. Trans by Zhang Ziqing. *Journal of Jianghan University*. Wuhan:
    Jianghan UP, 1015.

9 Poems in translation. *Poetry*. No. 1. Ed. Zhao Si. Beijing, China. 2018.

4 poems and discussion in Chinese. Zhang Ziqing. *A History of 20ᵗʰ Century American Poetry*. Volume II of III volumes. Beijing: 2018.

"River Rouge." *RESPECT: Poems About Detroit Music*. Ed. Jim Daniels and M. L. Liebler. East Lansing: Michigan State UP, 2020.

"Ukraine." *Busy Griefs, Raw Towns: a poetic response to the brutality of war in Ukraine*.

  Ed. G. F. Korreck. Grand Rapids: Schuler Books/Chapbook, 2022.

Journals

Big Scream, Blind Alley, In The Light, Windows in The Stone; Delirium; The World; Roof; Bombay Gin; New Blood; Ferro Botanica; Wonderland; The Grand Rapids Press; Long Shot; Action; Pay Up Dead Beat; Ahnoi; Planet Detroit; La Voz; The New York Quarterly; Lactuca; We; Big Fireproof Box; Big Hammer; Black Swan Review; Napalm Health Spa; Lame Duck; Vajra- dhatu Sun; Headcheck Number Four; Heaven Bone; Indefinite Space; Big Fish; Shambala Sun; The Wayne Literary Review; The Ann Arbor Poetry Forum; The Brooklyn Review; The Hazmat Review; Bill Freeman's Maga- zine; The Louisiana Review; Van Gogh's Ear; The Woodstock Journal; The Paterson Literary Review; Wildflowers: a Woodstock mountain poetry anthology; Presa; The Newark Review; Street Value #2; The Café Review; Contemporary International Literature (Beijing); "Completing a Life Circle: My Correspondence with Allen Ginsberg." Interview by Kirpal Gordon. *Taking Giant Steps*. Blog. (16 June 2016). Poetry Spoken Here (podcast interviews by Charlie Rossiter, 11 August 2016). Also: "Silent March Candle- light Vigil for George Floyd," "Alvin Ailey's Ode," "Hour of the Ghost Dance" and "Onward, as Creeley Used to Sign" in *Indefinite Space* and "Ukraine" and "Antietam" on the David Cope bio page. *Poets of the Planet*.

Online

The David Cope Papers 1907-2023. The University of Michigan Special
      Collections Resource Center. Ann Arbor: The University of
      Michigan Hatcher Graduate Library.
The Dave Cope Sampler. *The Museum of American Poetics*. Jim Cohn, curator.
The Oral History of Poetry in Grand Rapids. David Cope. Interviewed by
      Toni Bal. Christine Stephens Krieger, director.

Index of Titles

Note: Some poems have the same title, thus forming a brief series through time. The various versions are numbered in parentheses after each title.

A

The Abandoned	137
The Abandoned City	148
Abandoned Hotel	26
Abu Ghraib	244
Adieu à Jeff Because	314
After Lope	245
After Ronsard	225
After the Long, Hard Day	119
After the Polar Vortex	344
Alba: The Sailors	172
Albeniz, Sor, & Sanz	106
Alex Jane	100
all night	194
Alone	62
Alvin Ailey's Ode	357
American Dream	25
American Dream: The Fall of Saigon	4
American Pewter with Burroughs II	300
A Midnight Rose for Michael Pingarron	254
A Million Mute Corpses Speak	39
Among Daisies & Lily Blossoms	20
Among the Best Minds of His Generation	353
Andrey Voznesensky	289
Antietam	59
AP Wire Story: "Janitors at Risk"	136
April (1)	198
April (2)	294

A Quiet Life   27
Armstrong to Gothics   124
As My Mother Lay Waiting   261
At the Croyden   64
Audubon in Fog: The Descent   140

B

Baseball   50
Before I Leave for the Mountains   111
Below the Headlines   130
Between Sleep & Wake   268
Beyond the dream, the open door   352
Big Sale Shop, Bargains Galore   255
Birthday Dreams for Andy   373
The black bees   267
Blowout in Fast Traffic   92
Blue April   63
Blue Notes for New York   216
Blues for Frank   298
Bomb Fragments, Body Parts   218
The Breakwater   68
Burning Babies   40

C

Canyon Rim to Hopi Point Sunrise   228
Catch   80
Catching Nothing   143
CETA Office   43
A Charm   168
Chicago Springtime   358
Chinese Calligraphy   48
Chorus of Snores   113
CIA Manual Discovered   61
The City in Agony   256

Coming Home   126
Convent Garden   149
The Cranes   177
Crash   44
Cricket   61
The Crippled Doe   295
Crystal Lake to Beulah   274

D

Dawn Kayaking the Owashtanong   315
Death, you come   264
Desert Serenade   247
A Desperate Mother   354
Diné Woman   114
The Disappearing Sages   219
The dharma at last   212
Dreaming on You   18
A Dream of Jerusalem   272

E

Each Wound Became a Voodoo Mouth   158
Early Spring Morn Milwaukee   312
Easter   78
El Mozote   159
Emile at the Crossroads   290
The Empty Chair   279
Empty Street   31
End at the Beginning   319
End of the Shift   32
ER Saturday Night   214
Euclid Avenue   16
The Exchange   10

F

Fallen	263
Farewell	151
Fireball in the Clouds	127
The First Death	52
Flight to Paumanok: A Still Station	342
Flight to Phoenix	277
The Flood	76
For All Lost Love	156
for allen	174
For Anne at 70	326
For Antler, after the storm	301
For Billy	110
For Curt	306
For Fin & George	150
For Helen Cope	146
For Martin King	195
For Suzanne	104
For the Old Man's Tears	161
The Fourth	226
Fragile Moves	341
Frail Dreams	266
Fran	204
Free Clothes	199
From the Top Step of Guangde Temple	349
The Front Lines	131
Further Progress	69

G

The Gateless Gate	320
Getting the Pump Out	75
Ghazal for the Coming Spring	132
Ghazal of the High Plateau	208
Ghost Dance for *La Grande Vitesse*	162

The Gift   220
Gone (as you are)   221
Gone West   112
Ground Zero   217

H

Haditha   246
Happy Birthday: you'd be 99   285
Harvest Sundown   116
He took a long pull on the stout, thanked us all   180
Her New Room   269
the hidden meadow   192
Hostas   243
Hot Coals Burning on Your Tongue   93
Hour of the Ghost Dance   369

I

I, You, She or He   307
In a Sentimental Mood   227
In Fitful Sleep   129
In Heavy Clouds, In Cold Rain   154
In My Father's House   278
In Silence   215
In the Alley   181
Industrial Clinic   89
The Invisible Keys   90
Iran   96

J

January 6 Suite   361
The Job   182
July   115

K

Kali Yuga Super Blue Blood Moon	339
Killings to be Made in Soybean Futures	109

L

"La Goulue" Considers His Lines	232
Labor Day	51
Lamentations	5
Landlady, The	34
Landlady on the Stoop	67
A Language of Our Time	308
Last Look	271
Last of My Singing Fathers	252
Lear by Lanternlight	229
Leaves in Fall	324
leaving classes	191
Liberty Bell, The	60
The Lights of St. Ignace	82
long thin clouds	325
Lost Loves	203
Love in the Corona	360
The Lovers Sleep	166
Lunch Hour	45

M

Madadayo in Dreams	234
Mais où sont les neiges d'antan?	270
Manhattan from Jersey City	343
Many Reunions	187
March (1)	155
March (2)	291
A March Blessing	142
Marines with Cobbled Armor	248

Masks of Six Decades	240
May (1)	54
May (2)	251
May Song	321
Memorial Stone	84
Memory in Love	186
Memory's Balm	351
Midsummer Night	147
Midwinter Cleanup	73
Minneapolis Airport Delay	328
The Mirror of Heaven	178
Modern Art	58
Monday Morning	12
The Moon	347
Moonlight & Sunrise	86
Mottled Wings	77
The Mountain: Inauguration 2017	340
My Father	81

N

The New Foot	99
New Home	242
New Life	188
New Moon	102
New Windows	74
The Night Blooming Cereus	239
no time to feel	197

O

October Surprise: An Absurd Reverie	249
The Odor of Death	41
Old Man	108
The Old Stebbens Place	70
Old Woman in the Café Window	65

On Ramp at Rush Hour   97
On the Main Road   83
On the Road   13
Onward, as Creeley used to sign   366
Out thru the eye beyond the stars   236
Operating Instructions   11
Owashtanong Sunrise   222

P

Pacific Sundown   138
Paint Work   33
Party Talk   57
Passing Phantoms   368
Paterson Falls   14
Peace   36
The Plumber   35
Poem Beginning with a Line by Pound   160
Pointing It Up   135
A Prophecy   165
Push Off   184

Q

Quitting Time   21

R

The Rain   9
Rainy Dawn   98
Reading the Signs   207
Refugees   3
Reliving the News   6
The Return   123
Rexroth Gone   49
The Rhododendron   171
Rhubarb   79

The River 152

River Rouge 281

Rix is Gone 318

Roses 15

Rush Hour in the Swamp, Near Hopewell Mounds 250

S

Sanctuary 372

Satie & Dante 167

Sears Service Center Waiting Room 72

Seul Choix Shoreline, Owashtanong Dreams 257

Seven a.m. Buffing the Floor 19

She 292

The Shotgun 30

Sierra Madre & North to Oregon 139

Silent March Candlelight Vigil for George Floyd 359

sirens & flashing lights stop 176

Slagboom Tool & Die 42

Sleep 107

Soft Rain 85

Solihull to Marylebone 206

A Song for Our Lady 350

So the day begins 303

Spirit Walk Sunset 374

Starlight Call 262

Sunday Morning 134

Sundown 118

Sweeping 54

The Swimmer 276

T

Tahquamenon 280

"Take Care of Yourself" 66

Taylor Bridge to Pines Point 71

Tears   29
Tender Petals for Calm Crossing   210
"the weight of the world is love"   323
Thornapple   302
Thru Gary & Calumet to the Monet   183
Tiananmen Square Sequence   94
To the edge & back: the gift   241
Train Crossing   22
The Train: *Howl* in Chicago   329
Turning (1)   46
Turning (2)   196
Twenty Below   172
Two for Creeley   296
Two Hearted River   178
Two Women Dream Together   173

U

Ukraine   370
Unbidden Dream: a melancholy evening . . .   355
Until Love Is Equal   367
Up All Night   8

V

A View from the Road   38
A Vision in Manistique   189

W

Waiting for dawn in a Beijing hotel room   348
Waiting for The Clash   17
Washington   7
The Welfare Office   28
"What Thou Lovest Well"   157
the white bristled sallow face in the photo   224
White Light   153

Wild Calls in the Night   256
Will   105
Words   133
The Work   322
Wyrd Song   311

Y
Yeah, an' here he was   230

About David Cope

*

Born 1948, Detroit, Mi. Education: BA University of Michigan, MA+30 Western Michigan University. Married 54 years, 3 grown children. Taught Shakespeare, Drama, Creative Writing, Intro to Philosophy, Multicultural Literature, Women's Studies at Grand Rapids Community College for 22 years; adjunct faculty at Western Michigan University, taught Shakespeare 7 years; school custodian 18 years before that. Kent County Dyer Ives Poetry Competition, first place adult category winner, 1971, 1972. Pushcart Prize winner, 1977. Distinguished Alumni award, GRCC 1984. Award in literature from American Academy/Institute of Arts and Letters, 1988. Nine books and two chapbooks published. Editor and publisher, *Big Scream* magazine, 1974-2021 (60 issues). Poet Laureate of Grand Rapids, Mi. 2011-2014; editor of three anthologies: *Nada Poems* (Nada, 1988), *Sunflowers & Locomotives: Songs for Allen* (elegies for Allen Ginsberg, Nada, 1998), and *Song of the Owashtanong: Grand Rapids Poetry in the 21st Century* (Ridgeway, 2013). Recent publications include *The Train: "Howl" in Chicago* (chapbook, Multifarious Press, 2017), and *The Invisible Keys: New and Selected Poems 1975-2017* (Ghost Pony Press, 2018). David's "In Silence" appeared in Chinese translation by Professor Zhang Ziqing as part as group of 9-11 poems in *Houston Garden of Verses*, and nine of his poems were included in translations by Zhang in *Poetry Periodical* (Beijing). Dr. Peter Feng also translated two of Cope's poems for a Chinese online poetry journal, *Poetry Sky*. David's poems were translated and discussed in vol. II (1379-1386) of Professor Zhang's three volume study, *A History of 20ᵗʰ Century American Poetry*. Cope was the only American poet conferee at the Suining International Poetry Week and Chen Zi'ang Poetry Awards in Sichuan, China (March, 2019). His work from that journey appears in *A Bridge Across the Pacific: Leaves for Chen Zi'ang, Guan Yin, and Du Fu* (Jabber Publications, 2020). His "River Rouge" appears in *RESPECT: The Poetry of Detroit Music*, ed. Jim Daniels and M. L. Liebler (Michigan State University Press, 2020). In 2021, David published *The Correspondence of David Cope and Allen Ginsberg (1976-1996)* (Giant Steps Press). In 2025, Claire Durrand-Gasselin translated eight of his later poems into French, now out for pub-lication in Paris and elsewhere. The David Cope Papers are maintained at the University of Michigan Special Collections Resource Center, and his web-page, The Dave Cope Sampler, is online at the Museum of American Poetics.

Photo: David Cope editing *A Bridge Across the Pacific*, by Jon Dambacher (2019)

www.ingramcontent.com/pod-product-compliance
Lightning Source LLC
Chambersburg PA
CBHW081527120626
46550CB00009B/2640